People Fusion

Best Practices to Build and Retain a Strong Team

Mark Allen	Christie Engler
Lee Autore	Liz Flynn
Andrea Bjorkman	Cheryle Hays
Meghan Brown	Connor Hopkins
Rob Chambers	Mike Sipple, Jr.
James Cowan	Paul LaLonde
Angie Dodge	Bonita Palmer

Contents

Foreword

Steve Browne, | SHRM-SCP, Chief People
Officer at LaRosa's, Inc.,

We live in a world surrounded by humans. You will find yourself swimming in a sea of humanity everywhere you go. Chances are you are unfamiliar with who you're passing in a public place or who's joining you at a public event. Astonishingly, we are surrounded by many different people but only genuinely connected to a few. Sure, you may know a few people who have a significant number of people they're connected to, but they are indeed an exception.

Have you ever paused in one of these public settings and just looked around? You see people of different shapes, sizes, skin colors, appearances, languages, cultures, etc. Each person is facing something in their life. You're not aware of what it is. It may be something challenging, a deep concern about others, or they're experiencing immense joy on some level. I've always wanted to stop people and ask them: "What are you facing?" This may seem too bold a question, perhaps even intrusive, but the idea of getting to know who they are, what they're facing, and how they're maneuvering through life fascinates me.

This landscape closely mirrors what we all find ourselves in during work, especially in the world of human resources.

Every company is filled with those we know very little about, if we are honest about it. We may know some demographic information like where they live, their family situation, and how long they've been with the company. There may be a handful of people with whom we regularly interact, which allows us to know each other even more, but there's no guarantee. Most conversations are about the work, not the PEOPLE DOING the WORK.

We need to have a method and focus that more intentionally brings everyone together. We need to create a *"People Fusion"*!!

Fusion, by definition, is "the process or result of joining two or more things together to form a single entity." (Oxford Languages)[1] Bringing people together in an organizational environment is daunting and challenging because people tend to keep (what they deem is) a safe distance from each other and may not see the need and value in coming together. In today's reset work environment, the need for people-centric companies is a necessity. I would go so far as to state that if companies don't take the time to become "people-first" oriented, then they will cease to be relevant going forward.

Becoming a people-first company is difficult because HR pros face decades of tradition and methods that people continue to cling to despite being ineffective for years. Thankfully, the astute authors in this book have created and cultivated a series of solid ideas, concepts, and approaches that you can utilize to foster a tangible PEOPLE FUSION throughout your company. Each chapter adds a new facet to consider and implement, which will equip you to shape, create and form a culture that calls for people to come together. It doesn't take away from any person's individuality. On the contrary, it ALLOWS for uniqueness and individuality to bloom and flourish and then gives you the means to weave everyone's unique talent and strengths into a viable fabric of an effective, people-fused company.

I'm sure you'll take this book and keep it as a ready reference and resource as you take the steps toward people fusion. The time for people to come together is now !!

Notes

1. "Fusion." Fusion Noun - Definition, Pictures, Pronunciation and Usage Notes | Oxford Advanced Learner's Dictionary at OxfordLearnersDictionaries.com, https://www.oxfordlearnersdictionaries.com/us/definition/english/fusion#:~:text=%2F%CB%88fju%CB%90%CA%92n%2F-,%2F%CB%88fju%CB%90%CA%92n%2F,things%20together%20to%20form%20one.

I.

Burned Out or Fired Up?

Ways to Turn Burnout into Stronger Teams, Talent, and Organization

Meghan Brown | Transformation and Career Coach, Consultant

What is burnout?

What if you could successfully transform your employees, your teams, and yourself for greater impact?

Burnout is a hot topic and an issue that needs immediate solutions to restore our employees, teams, and organizations. Psychology Today describes "Burnout" as "a state of emotional, mental and often physical exhaustion brought on by prolonged or repeated stress in work and/ or life."[1] In the realm of work, stress happens when the approach to work, or the work itself, conflicts with a person's values and preferred way of working. Along with this type of stress, I'm also seeing coaching clients who, now burned out and wanting to quit, are asking questions about who they are and what they really want to do/be. Derek Thompson introduced the concept of workism, where he describes people's view of their jobs as – not only – an economic necessity, but also as the core of one's identity and purpose.[2] He goes on to say this way of thinking is making Americans miserable. With this combination of both stress from a fast-paced, high workload environment and employee's identity struggle, it sets the stage for tough problems for people, teams, and organizations to solve. It's leaving many with stress that leads to and causes exhaustion as well as an inability to cope.

Already exhausted and overwhelmed employees continue to work hard which could lead to more serious health concerns for those employees while others are disengaging from the work, team, and company as a result of burnout. In a recent study by joblist.com of 19,000 workers, 49% of workers indicated that they felt the burn out (Gupta, 2022). Many are staying in their jobs due to fears associated with the economy and job market. Burned out employees are stressed and exhausted which makes for disengaged employees. As a result, we are seeing the full picture of burnout where a large portion of your workforce may be either exhibiting behaviors leading to burnout or they have worked themselves into a stage of feeling actively burned out. Whether you/your employees are on the path to burnout or are already burned out, it's a big, complex problem for both employees and organizations to address now.

Five Organizational Problems to Solve

We've got to solve both the organizational and personal problems of our employees. Organizations are tasked with solving five key problems when it comes to addressing burnout:

1. Unfair treatment at work
2. Unmanageable workload
3. Lack of role clarity
4. Lack of communication and support from managers
5. Unreasonable time pressures[3]

Without addressing these issues, organizations will continue to see the impact in lower engagement scores, higher attrition, average tenure numbers dropping, declining customer service, or external customer metrics dropping. Talented people leave, organizational knowledge exits the business, and teams and managers are left to struggle with the additional workload. With the attrition due to burnout, teams and managers feel it, taking on the work in their roles and jobs, introducing change and more work to the employees and managers left behind, which leads to more burnout. It becomes a vicious cycle. Over time, profitability drops.The cost of not addressing burnout is high and rising.

While companies are working to address these monumental problems over time, understand the impact and get to the root problem to determine and scale solutions, it begs the question, 'What solution can help NOW?'. Organizations need innovative solutions that can calm the flames of burnout for their employees **today**. There needs to be great consideration for the employees that are burned out and need help **NOW**! Employees are desperate for immediate solutions.

Existing Solutions

In partnership with the organization, employees have existing options to manage burnout and its impact:

1. They can work with their managers and leaders to solve the individual and/or organizational problems.
2. They can work through their own causes of stress and exhaustion (that are within their control) through the organization's Employee Assistance/Counseling benefit.

Independently, employees can work with their own counselor, primary health physicians and/or consider getting a coach. All of these options can positively impact an employee and the organization; depending on the level of burnout and the specific problems to address.

An Immediate Innovative Solution

As a career and encouragement coach, I've seen the power of coaching transform individuals from feeling burned out to fired up. This is happening consistently, so it's important for both organizations **AND** individuals to consider this as an immediately implementable, effective, and innovative solution **TODAY**!

How it Works

I'd like to share a recent example where safe, trusting and objective coaching conversations transformed an employee from burnout to being fired up. First, let me describe the process of a coaching conversation. These types of conversations help someone to see where they are, where they want to go, and to make the plans to see themselves clearly and arrive at a better place.

Powerful Coaching Conversations & Process

This is a general approach for coaching conversations and a way to talk through how you/your employees can get outside the box of burnout for work, work roles, and life. It follows a common coaching procedure which you can use for coaching yourself or for coaching others. If burnout has you or your team feeling diminished, without energy, and uninspired to find solutions, these questions for self discovery and problem solving can help to uncover your personal opportunities. They will leave room to allow you to think differently, learn and grow in a way that supports your health, and brings more joy and happiness to your work and life.

Three considerations/steps:

Step 1: What's on your mind? With a trusted friend or colleague, talk through what's on your mind, how you are feeling about work and life and why you might be feeling that way.

Tell me more. Have a friend or colleague repeat back to you what you said. Write down what you are feeling and any problems you shared. Edit or add anything to create a clearer, more descriptive picture.

Step 2: What's the idea look like? With your friend or on your own, user your imagination to paint the ideal picture of your life. Paint the picture of your life as you'd like it to be. Consider all aspects. If there is an area of your life where you are feeling particularly burned out or uninspired, try and get as specific as you can. Write it down. You might ask yourself some questions like:

- What have I always wanted to do?
- What would I be doing if I was truly utilizing my strengths (at work or in life)? Don't know your strengths? I highly recommend taking the strengths-finder test to identify your top five strengths; you will also be provided with a description.[4] Identifying your top five strengths will bring you back to what it looks and feels like when you are at your best!
- What do you value and why? How does that look/how do you **_want_** it to look in your life? (You can do this online![5]
- What do I want to do more of?
- What do I want to try and why?
- What are the things I really enjoy?
- When thinking of your ideal future self, how will you think, feel, look, or make decisions differently than you do today?

Step 3: What actions can you take today to align with your ideal or better self/life? Consider your options or ways you can get closer to what you want/that ideal. If brainstorming solutions is not your strength, you can engage a friend in this part, too. Try and list out ideas here objectively without judgment on "good" ideas or "bad" ones. Simply think of what could help you get to that ideal as potential options. Then look at that list and think about which one you'd like to do. Does it need to be broken down into smaller steps? Determine what those small steps are that you can do with the energy that you have. Decide how you are going to make time to take those steps, and why it's important to you (more important than other priorities that might creep in on your time/focus).

Then you get to take action and go do that thing! There may be something that gets in the way of taking actionable steps. Something that is keeping you from making the time. In this case, you might need to examine what's getting in the way and think through how you might make a plan/commitment to overcome that obstacle or barrier.

Repeat steps one through five and remember to give yourself the grace to learn and grow from what is discovered. Celebrate big and small wins along the way!

Before you know it, that burnout you _**were**_ feeling will start to shift and you'll find yourself feeling more alive, more yourself, more empowered, more engaged, and more energetic. With more energy, you can take more actions and you _will_ see more progress. You will undoubtedly inspire others!

An Example of How Coaching Addresses Burnout with Personalized Solutions

Here's an example of how going through these five steps for identifying burnout worked out for one young man in particular. This professional had worked in the banking industry for more than ten years. He went from feeling burned out to developing himself and getting ready for the next best thing. His three considerations/steps looked like this:

Step 1: What's on your mind? *I've been in this role for a very long time and after a promotion a couple years ago, realized that I don't enjoy doing this job anymore. It's not only the type of work that I'm doing, it's the amount of work that is expected of me and the unrealistic deadlines which have me working at home at night on top of the work I complete in the office. I want/need a new job as soon as possible, but realistically three to six months.*

> **...Anything you'd like to add to that around what you'd like to do more of or see more of in your life? Can something be better or what's missing?** *In addition to all that, I know I can add value to my life by creating a new tool, but I don't have the time. I also know my team can do more, but I worry about the*

quality of work we will deliver if I'm not involved in everything.

Step 2: ...Tell me more. What's the ideal look like? *I've always wanted to create that new tool and have told a few of my managers and mentors about it over the years. There has always been great support for it and the value it could provide was clear and acknowledged. In the ideal world, my team would deliver quality and accurate work without my constant oversight so that I could have more time to do the things that I love. This includes my hobbies and spending more quality time with my wife and kids.* **(Notice the ideal/ shift to a positive goal, vision or outcome and capture it.)** The shift I heard was from the original presenting problem/ solution of feeling burned out/needing a new job to a vision of **leading** his team effectively to deliver quality through **delegation to get greater work/life balance?** If you don't see it, it's a coaching skill of listening that you can grow over time. I shared his stated vision and goal back to him to be able to discuss it and make sure it's clear, concise, and accurate.

Step 3: What can you do to get closer to that ideal? *Well, I was planning to meet with my mentor as well as a colleague that works in another company. They know about the tool I want to create, so talking to them* **AND** *communicating that I would love the opportunity to do the work to create the tool would be something I can do this week. I'm also hiring a new manager that can support me in getting our team to deliver higher quality work and if I can delegate some of my current workload to this new manager, that would help a lot, too. I* can hire a new analyst and also start to transfer some of my organizational knowledge, as well. So, ideally, they will be able to step in to help in a more robust and meaningful way.

1. My next step is meeting with my colleague at another bank. I can schedule that for Thursday, as we just emailed about potential dates.
2. I'll reach out to my mentor, too, for dates in two weeks.
3. The new manager starts in a few weeks so that will have to wait for now.

Repeating the Steps to Continuously Address Burnout

Most people who deal with burnout should understand that there are things that get in the way with seeing progress quickly. This one might sound familiar to you and that was definitely the case for this person. In our second coaching session, he shared what's getting in the way and really causing more burnout – BACK TO BACK MEETINGS! (Sound familiar?...)

So, in this case, we went back to his goals of leadership and delegation and walked through the process of step 1 through step 3 once again. After determining more small steps to grow in the areas identified in going through the steps again, he's delegating more and feeling better about work. Also, as he networked, he's getting more visibility to job options. The real win in this story is the renewed sense of confidence and the fresh perspective from the process of making time to understand the root problems of burnout and talking through ways to solve them with goals and next steps towards those goals. It feels good to make progress, getting beyond the fear and newness, to get to a better place of being productive, empowered and excited about your life/direction.

The company is also retaining this talented individual in the meantime **AND** benefitting from some next steps like transferring certain knowledge to the team in case he does leave. The coaching process fuels people to be happy with their current circumstances while working on making those circumstances better, making themselves better, and making their lives better.

An Innovative Coaching Solution

There is an innovative solution here for organizations if we are able to combine providing access to a coach, dedicated time, and a safe environment for those conversations along with openness and partnership for employee growth. It becomes a **WIN** for the employee at work, a **WIN** for the teams they're on, and a **WIN** for the organization and the world. It seems like there may even be a few more wins in there!

Here's what an innovation coaching solution might look like in action. A company would have a designated space, time, and specific coaching available each week for employees to engage with the coach directly in conversations and/or to continue to work on their plans for growth (set up in previous coaching conversations). To create that safe space, it might be a company café. It might include light snacks and drinks while people work on themselves/their goals.

Another Example Where Coaching Uniquely Addresses Burnout Getting an Employee Fired Up

This real example shows how an employee got connected to a coach through a recommendation from a friend. They were provided with a safe space and an objective listener to partner with for coaching. The coach helped to identify personal challenges to solve. The employee was able to consider new options and plan for a more fun, happier, healthier life. Here's an overview of her three steps:

Step 1: What's on your mind? This employee, like many, came to me ready to quit her job that very day. Of course she can do that, but we sat down in a local coffee shop and I asked her to tell me what was going on first and to help me understand what she was experiencing at work (Step 1). She shared in great detail about how the pressure to reach high performance metrics, even through the Covid-19 Pandemic, was causing her a large amount of stress. In fact, she was even fearful of having a heart attack – which was driving the top voiced solution of quitting her job today.

- I asked her to tell me more. It's the sales side that is draining her and she doesn't want to do it anymore. She's a high achiever and works to meet her goals and often exceeds them. Her high performance comes at the cost of working too many long hours and working more than she wants to work but she cannot stop short of meeting/exceeding those sales metrics. She wants to find a job outside of sales that aligns to her strengths, pay expectations, values, and experience.

Step 2: What's a better job/life look like for you? Let's envision a life outside of sales and the challenges it brings and what that would mean for your way of working and life (Step 2). She explained that she loves the people in the company and one particular aspect of her job with research. She loves her team, and the collaboration across the business to get work done and coaching/developing people as their team leader. We talked through her values using a values exercise. You can do this online here if you'd like to give it a try.[6] I recommend that everyone know their strengths and values as foundational exercises to know/ define yourself and align your life to it.

- (Tell me more)...I asked her to share some options to get her closer to her ideal place and role. She shared that she could start networking in the organization and with people she knew in similar companies in town.

Step 3: What can you do today to reach that better life/ work experience/job? For this step, she chose to start meeting with a few key people she knew well in the company who were leading teams that aligned better to her strengths, values, and experience and where she could see herself develop and grow and add value to the company/ across the business by bringing her passion. She also met with leaders she enjoyed working with in the past to see what opportunities were out there. She probably had more than ten conversations internally, which did a few things:

- helped leaders know she was looking for a new role
- helped them to see/hear what she wanted to do and where she could add value
- got leaders thinking about how they could keep her vs. lose her based on hearing the passion to find a new opportunity inside the company

In our third and last coaching session (in only a few months' time), she shared that the company had created the perfect role for her. Her ideal world/role is now on the table and she's fired up. As if that weren't enough, she reflected on her experience and decided she does not want burnout to happen to her again. She recognized that she can control the likelihood of burnout by being aware of how much she is working, taking breaks, setting boundaries, and being a good example of balance for others. She also determined that she needed to set more realistic deadlines for herself with her work.

I love and am honored that story after story of coaching conversations have these happy endings: a few safe, trusting and honest conversations were key and necessary in order to identify root problems and letting creative, unique individuals develop solutions that work for them and their goals for work and life. It's inspiring. Burnout is deeper than you can even begin to believe; it can be seen and heard once an individual decides to open up and share their perceptions of their work, their role, their job, and how it's impacting them. Initially, they are feeling such a high degree of stress that they felt there was no other option than to give up and leave their current job or role.

> "Employee burnout is personal – individuals have unique problems to solve to address their burnout which is what makes coaching, which enables someone to identify and solve their own problems, a versatile and empowering solution."

The solutions to burnout are as unique as the people themselves. So, while organizations need to continue to work on systemic and structural solutions, **solely** doing so doesn't address the unique, personal solutions for each specific employee. Burnout is **personal**. Therefore, each employee needs a personalized approach. I believe coaching delivers that personalization and companies need to provide access to coaching for associates now as burnout.

Barriers to Coaching Solutions

1. Coaching is new to the organization as a service and a key core competency. Each company needs to address this if they are to be successful in incorporating coaching to combat burnout.
2. Openness to coaching as a viable solution to burnout. This can be a barrier at both the organizational and individual level. For coaching to work, organizations and individuals need to buy in and engage with coaches

and the coaching process.

3. Another barrier to companies and individuals embracing coaching is the cost. We are in the age and level of urgency that burnout needs coaching as a solution at the benefit-level. What I mean by that is: just like healthcare, just like 401ks, employees need to be able to talk through their current work-state with a trusted partner and come to their own solutions and accountability. There is a cost to calculate in offering coaching to all employees.

So, if companies embraced this innovative solution for the benefit of both their employees and their organizations, what could that look like for companies and what would it cost to invest in this type of solution?

Calculating the Investment in a Solution

Embracing these coaching solutions would be at the cost of providing a coach on site for a set number of hours a month, the space to host those employees, food or drinks and any additional content or programming. The space would be where employees can gather in groups to work on their plans, meet with the coach, and also get guidance on a few foundational activities for them to be able to guide their own lives and shift from burnout to fired up (values, strengths and vision). The cost would vary based on the coach's hourly or program/content fees. The prices could also vary based on the number of employees participating and if you'd like to set up a portion of this cost where the employee would pay. In the future, I envision this could be set up similar to a health benefit. No matter what the choice on cost is, it is a small price to pay for a huge return on investment for your people, their potential, teams, retention and the culture of your company. This is truly invaluable when new studies are showing the organizations and economical impact of burnout are extremely high.

The Cost of NOT Addressing Burnout

A blog summarizing the financial impact shared, "In a 2020 survey from Spring Health, 76% of American workers reported experiencing burnout. While Harvard Business Review estimates that the annual healthcare spending due to workplace burnout is anywhere from $125 billion to $190 billion. Gallup also found burned-out employees cost $3,400 out of every $10,000 in salary because they are disengaged in their work. We're talking about high turnover and lower productivity. And replacing workers is expensive. The replacement cost for the average worker is one-half to two times the annual salary."[7]

Time is money and organizations are going to need time to address some major factors causing burnout if they want to remain profitable and continue to grow and succeed. I've seen many companies addressing burnout through more marketing of the employee assistance programs. This is a great benefit as we need to continue to encourage employees to get the help they need at the first signs of burnout.

Goal: Shifting from Burnt Out to Fired Up

We all want engaged employees. We all want loyal employees. We all want happy employees. We all want inspired, energetic, clear, and healthy leaders. We all want people to want to stay at the company because they have great work to do, a great manager, and are proud of the organization in which they work. It is absolutely imperative that people are excited about their work, their team, and what they get to do and accomplish. We **need** people that catch others on fire with the vision and impact they can make through their work. We want to be those employees and leaders that are fired up! This has to happen **NOW.**

Impact

When employees go from burned out to "fired up," engagement increases, people stay. Customer satisfaction and profitability is not impacted by burnout when employees have a healthy relationship with their work and in their lives. It is also vital that they are **happy**.

We can address burnout if we get curious about it and work

with employees to change their perception of their jobs, tasks, and how they are being carried out or being asked to carry out. We need to engage with employees to understand where they are and want to be and invite them to consider ways they can change things up when their job/role is in conflict with their values, the way they'd like to work or if it's in conflict with who they are and want to be or become.

What's exciting about this is that personal elements of burnout (and ongoing prevention) are things individuals can solve when they ask themselves about their approach to work, how they'd like their strengths and values to play out, and consider who they are and want to be or become. This perspective brings burnout to a level where individuals can truly and clearly see the problems – or needs – and think of solutions to create more fun and better overall health and happiness in their work and personal/home life. A new fire is lit and a fresh, bright light shines within that employee and they carry it through to their work and in their lives. That's exciting and it's transforming individuals from burnout to being fired up!

Getting Started with Coaching Solutions

How can you get fired up and think outside of the box of burnout? As an individual, you can explore getting a coach. It's an innovative approach which creates a safe space for you.

As an organization, if you are looking for a return on your investment that meets all employees needs, with transformative impact in the short term, there is a solution to address burnout – explore and activate coaching. It's an innovative and less costly approach is to create a safe space for you and your employees to be in the driver's seat of their future and have conversations that intrinsically motivate them and activate their problem solving skills. Remember: it's all about your/employee's perspective on work and sense of self. You and your employees will be able to see, address, and take action to address personal burnout challenges and be able to immediately see and have your own individual story or employees' stories of exciting growth and transformation.

What if we gave employees and teams something that would make it easy to reduce, recover, and prevent burnout? Prevention and progress through problem solving enables employees to do the important work? As organizations work on long-term complex solutions, let's consider how we might bring the transformative power of coaching to more organizations and employees to get them from burnout to being fired up about work and life.

Interested in or excited about innovative or coaching solutions to fight burnout and ways to get yourself, your team or organization fired up? Contact Meghan Brown for more information!

Notes

1. "Burnout." Psychology Today, Sussex Publishers, https://www.psychologytoday.com/us/basics/burnout.

2. Thompson, Derek. "Workism Is Making Americans Miserable." The Atlantic, Atlantic Media Company, 13 Aug. 2019, https://www.theatlantic.com/ideas/archive/2019/02/religion-workism-making-americans-miserable/583441/.

3. Agrawal, Ben Wigert and Sangeeta. "Employee Burnout, Part 1: The 5 Main Causes." Gallup.com, Gallup, 2 Dec. 2022, https://www.gallup.com/workplace/237059/employee-

burnout-part-main-causes.aspx.

4. "Top 5 Cliftonstrengths: En-US - Gallup." Gallup Store, 2022,
   https://store.gallup.com/p/en-us/10108/
   top-5-cliftonstrengths.

5. says:, Kumary Sirikumara, et al. "Live Your Core Values:
   10-Minute Exercise to Increase Your Success." TapRooT®
   Root Cause Analysis, 28 Nov. 2022,
   https://www.taproot.com/live-your-core-values-exercise-
   to-increase-your-success/.

6. says:, Kumary Sirikumara, et al. "Live Your Core Values:
   10-Minute Exercise to Increase Your Success." TapRooT®
   Root Cause Analysis, 28 Nov. 2022,
   https://www.taproot.com/live-your-core-values-exercise-
   to-increase-your-success/.

7. "The Real Cost of Burnout - on Your People and Your Bottom
   Line ." Pavilion, 4 May 2022, https://www.joinpavilion.com/
   blog/the-real-cost-of-burnout.

Meghan Brown

Meghan has over twenty years of experience in growing innovation and leadership by creating and delivering fun, personalized individual and group programs and coaching. Meghan's passion is to help big and small companies, and schools see transformational results through personal and organizational outcomes from coaching. With coaching programs, we can tap into the amazing and unique value that individuals possess through the encouragement and permission to more confidently show, grow, and bring their most powerful skills and goals to life.

With the pace at which organizations are moving and changing along with COVID driving individuals to more self discovery of who they are and what really matters to them, it's no surprise that individuals within local companies like dunnhumbyUSA, Children's Hospital, Fifth Third Bank,

MedPace, The Cincinnati Zoo, Ipsos, 84.51 and more have reached out to Meghan over the years in search of help. The common theme of these requests is, "I don't feel heard, seen, or fulfilled – I'm burned out. I don't know what to do and I want to quit." Meghan works with individuals and organizations to shift from burnout to feeling fired up, which is what fuels better cultures and career paths! With Meghan's personalized and encouraging coaching programs, individuals and organizations can invest a little time to get a transformational return on people's lives and livelihood. This is a major win for greater engagement and healthy retention. More importantly, great coaching supports inspired, happier and healthier lives of employees and managers.

Meghan is also an inventor, writer, and mother to an amazing teenager, Aiden, and always working on growing and practicing her faith.

Connect with Meghan Brown:

https://www.linkedin.com/in/meghanbrown1/

mbinnovates@gmail.com or mbc3solutions@gmail.com

2.

The Philosopher Manager

Ancient Wisdom for Modern Opportunities

Paul A. LaLonde / HR Professional, SHRM-CP, Founding Consultant & Thought Coach at HR Logic, LLC.

> *"To be a philosopher is not merely to have subtle thoughts, nor even to found a school... it is to solve some of the problems of life, not only theoretically, but practically." – Henry David Thoreau*

In high school, I used to sit on the back porch with my grandpa. He'd smoke his cigar and sip his ginger ale. He did most of the talking, and I did most of the listening. He'd discuss life, how he dropped out of the seminary to marry my grandma (thank goodness for me!), or how – as a big time St. Louis Cardinals fan – he loved watching Stan "the Man"

Musial and Bob Gibson. One day during our time together, he turned to me and said, "Paul, you're a thinker."

It's true. I think a lot. My Predictive Index behavioral assessment, which is similar to a Myers Briggs or DISC assessment, states I "like to think things through" before moving forward towards solutions on major issues, with plans, and actions. I like to strategize to ensure I can move forward with the best possible course of action.

This conversation with my grandpa opened my eyes and forever changed me. This conversation is where the seeds were planted and flourished into eventual love of philosophy.

Many articles discuss how there is a skills gap in the workforce, and successful organizations need to figure out how to bridge that skills gap[1] . Many skills listed repeatedly include:

- Critical thinking
- Problem solving
- Innovation
- Communication
- Self-management

These skills, seemingly, are in short supply. Why? It may be partially intentional. I once overheard someone remark "Do managers think?" I thought to myself, "Do you want them to?"

The American education system may not be focusing on

the right things. There is a Twitter account called "@rebelEducator," and they posted a thought-provoking thread[2] where they list out the following skills that are not emphasized in most educational settings:

1. Criticallly reading
2. How to write – well
3. How to ask great questions
4. How to work in public
5. People skills, like relatability, awareness, and persuasion
6. How to find and create opportunities
7. How to become an expert at something

Notice an overlap? Many of these items are the same or possess similar skills that most organizations list as being part of the "skills gap" we're all trying to overcome![3]

So much success for organizations depends on managers and supervisors – those in people-leader positions. [4] Unfortunately, organizations often place folks into roles and situations without adequately preparing or helping them along the way. These leaders are unsure what to do, and therefore don't act as they should; if they even act at all! Being unsure of how to act or behave in new situations is normal, and it doesn't have to be to the detriment of organizations. Organizations should make it clear that it is okay to be unsure about what to do, but it is imperative for organizations to equip their people with the skills and abilities to **_figure out_** what to do when they are unsure. This is the difference between growth, stagnation, or something worse – like failure, closure, high turnover, etc.

Organizations need to teach their leaders how to think, and this begins with philosophy. Philosophy can be the catalyst pursuit in business (and life in general) between growth or irrelevance.

My journey into philosophy began over a decade ago when I was in a professional and personal rut. I felt lost and unsure about where I was headed or what I believed. I felt that my emotions had led me astray, or worse, hadn't been helping me understand what I wanted to be or where I wanted to go. Thankfully, I randomly picked up *The Art of Living: The Classical Manual on Virtue, Happiness, and Effectiveness* while perusing a local bookstore. Nowhere on the book cover did it mention "philosophy." In fact, the author was Epictetus. I didn't even know how to pronounce Epictetus, let alone know who they were! However, I needed help understanding "living" at the time, and the book was in the bargain section, so I figured **"Why not give it a try?!"**

As I read the introduction, I discovered that the book was based on Stoic philosophy. It turned out to be a modern translation of *The Enchiridion*, which was an ancient collection of teachings by Epictetus, a Roman slave turned Stoic philosopher. Particularly influential to me was Epictetus's thoughts on the true meaning of philosophy, which is captured in the following passage:

"True philosophy doesn't involve exotic rituals, mysterious liturgy, or quaint beliefs. Nor is it just abstract theorizing and analysis. It is, of

course, the love of wisdom. It is the art of living a good life."[5]

According to Epictetus's logic, philosophy is meant for everyone. Philosophy is meant to be a practical tool for everyday people to use as a guide for a happy life. It is important to note that "happy" in the ancient context isn't to be interpreted as "pleasure" – that's a modern translation. In the ancient world, a happy life is a "flourishing" life. To flourish in life, because business is a part of life, happiness is acting virtuously in all situations.

Now, specifically, in Epictetus's mind, his philosophy of Stoicism is meant for everyone. However, I extend this to **all** philosophy! Find what works for you – Stoicism, modernism, Taoism, African philosophy, nihilism – and apply it to your way of doing business. That way you always have a compass to find your direction in times when you don't know how to proceed! And that's the point! Philosophy is meant to be actionable. As Epictetus stated,

> *"Philosophy is intended for everyone, and it is authentically practiced only by those who wed it with action in the world toward a better life for all."* [6]

Yes, we must study it, but what good is that if it's not then put into action after it's been thoroughly studied? If we don't become better? If we don't find answers to complicated situations?

Philosophy is meant to be actionable. Leaders need to take action.

If you've seen *The Matrix* you will hopefully understand this analogy. Plato is one of the greatest philosophers in not only Western history, but in all of history. His seminal work is *The Republic*. In it, he puts forth the "Allegory of the Cave." The allegory goes that there are men imprisoned in a cave that are chained facing a wall and cannot move. They've been there for their entire lives, and know only the wall. This wall shows shadows of events going on behind them – people who cross the light cast these shadows and this is reality to the men. However, this reality isn't true; it's only what they see. Eventually, the best of those enslaved end up escaping their chains and leaving the cave, thus being exposed to the light of the Sun and true reality. If they stay in the outside world, the true world, they become enlightened and, subsequently, philosophers. Those who cannot take the truth present in the outside world go back into the cave towards the untruth and willfully become prisoners again.

Image 1: Plato's Allegory of the Cave[7]

In Plato's mind, philosophers, those who escaped the cave and found true understanding, were the only appropriate individuals who could or should lead others. He called them "Philosopher Kings." According to Plato, philosophers had the following characteristics making them worthy of being leaders:

- Undying love of wisdom and philosophy
- Selflessness, intelligence, reliability
- Willingness to live a simple life
- Using their status, knowledge, virtue to **HELP** others
- Pursuing virtue and goodness for their own sake and not for any rewards[8]

I think these are pretty strong characteristics for any organizational leader or manager to have! Plato said "States will never be happy until rulers become philosophers or philosophers become rulers."

Again, I believe applying philosophical principles and actions can give businesses an edge in helping their managers provide better leadership for themselves and their employees, as well as strengthen the organization as a whole. This is where my idea of the "Philosopher Manager" comes into play. In order for this to be accomplished, you must take Plato's concept of the "Philosopher King" and apply it to workplace leaders. Organizations will never be happy until managers become philosophers or philosophers become managers.

A quick note on "happiness." Like Plato, I used the ancient definition of the word, not the modern notion. In the modern context, happiness is often linked directly with pleasure and feeling good. These things are part of the equation, but not necessary for true happiness in the ancient sense; which can be thought of as a "flourishing life." Living a life that is thriving, prosperous, or growing – this is happiness. Aren't the best businesses thriving and growing? Happy organizations are flourishing organizations, and philosophy can be the path for this growth.

How does one become a "Philosopher Manager"? Through the realization and acceptance of Epictetus's claim that philosophy is for everyone. If you believe that philosophy is truly for everyone, then you are already a philosopher. If you think, read, question, and act then, whether you know it or not, you are already a philosopher. Philosophy isn't so much about coming up with grand ideas and answers to life's greatest questions as much as it's about developing a process to answer life's smaller day-to-day questions and come up with solutions for life's situations. It's about developing reason and logic. It's about thinking through a situation and coming up with your own processes for solving problems. Many times, this involves thinking differently than most people. Other times, it's coming to the same conclusion others have already come to. Every time, however, it's about using what you have inside you to determine what you know is ethical, just, or appropriate. It requires thinking through the problem and applying logic.

How would you identify a "Philosopher Manager"? What characteristics should one focus on to develop their ability to lead in a flourishing manner or way? Or in a way that fosters growth?

First, and foremost, is virtue. In many philosophical traditions, virtue and happiness are synonymous. One cannot be happy (flourishing) without virtue, which is "the highest good."[9] Behaving according to high moral standards. All virtue emanates from these Cardinal Virtues:

1. **Wisdom** – Diogenes said wisdom is "the knowledge of things good and evil and of what is neither good nor evil...knowledge of what we ought to choose, what we ought to beware of, and what is indifferent." Wisdom informs our actions. American business leader and educator Steven Covey said, "Between stimulus and response there is a space. In that space is our power to choose our response." In that space is your opportunity.

2. **Temperance** – Temperance is the knowledge that enough is enough. One needn't desire more than is necessary, nor that which isn't essential. Temperance is "self-control," which takes discipline. Aristotle thought of it as the "golden mean." Temperance can be found in the middle, somewhere between excess and deficiency.

3. **Courage** – Epictetus said two words should remain in one's mind "persist" and "resist." Doing what must be done despite the fear. Resisting the comfort of the status quo and coming to one's own judgment despite the external pressure to stay the same for fear of judgement. Courage to face misfortune, to risk oneself

for the sake of another. Or, as Ryan Holiday put it, "Courage to hold to your principles, even when others get away with or are rewarded for disregarding theirs. Courage to speak your mind and insist on the truth."

4. **Justice** – Marcus Aurelius said that justice is "the source of all the other virtues." In the ancient context justice is much broader than how we see it in the legal sense today. Sympatheia – the belief in mutual interdependence among everything in the universe; we are all one. Hurt someone else and you hurt yourself. Doing the right thing is to always do no harm to another.

While virtue is the most important possession of a "Philosopher Manager," virtue is nothing without reason and logic. Utilizing reason and logic is having knowledge of what you know, what you don't know, and how to use it – even when to use virtue or when it is not being used. Reason and logic stem from experience, exercising your brain as a muscle the same way a body builder hits the weights in order to strengthen, build, and maintain. The more you think, the better you think. The more you read, the more you learn about your thinking, how other people think, and how to challenge your own perceptions. Without reason and logic, virtue is naked. Mastering reasoning is to master yourself. It is to perform your duty, and it is to learn how to think clearly while being free from blinding perceptions.

A "Philosopher Manager" must care about others. This is woven into the character of all great leaders. Leading oneself is the first part; the first step. However, being able to lead others is what completes the cycle. One cannot lead others without truly being invested in the wellbeing of those they lead. Caring can only be the result of curiosity and non-judgement. We should be curious about our folks. What makes them tick? What are their dreams? Where do they want to go in their careers? Once you find the answers to those questions, don't judge them for it! Help them to achieve their goals, instead. Don't assume they can or cannot do certain things. Give them tasks to prove themselves one way or another. Ultimately, it's providing them a landing strip to land the plane. If they cannot, then it's on them, but don't put barriers up artificially or unnecessarily. This mindset takes kindness but remember that being kind is not the same thing as being nice. I always use the example – hopefully this example is not too alarming! – that it was the kind thing to do to put Old Yeller down once he got rabies. It was certainly not nice doing it! Let's hope that it never comes to this, but a comparable example is terminating folks. It is never nice to do so. It sucks! Yet, it could be the best, kindest thing one could do.

Finally, while a "Philosopher Manager" is resolute in their principles and virtues, they are not above changing their mind or changing their direction or course when and if needed. Bruce Lee isn't necessarily known for philosophy as much as his martial arts films, but he was a major philosopher. His philosophy can be summed up in these simple words:

> "Empty your mind. Be formless, shapeless, like
> water. You put water into a cup, it becomes the

cup. *You put water into a bottle, it becomes the bottle. You put it into a teapot, it becomes the teapot. Now water can flow or it can crash. Be water, my friend."*

This philosophical approach should be thought of as an embodiment of the qualities of water – embracing its fluidity; which can ultimately help us with the fluidity of life. As Bruce Lee said, "The good life is a process, not a state of being. It is a direction, not a destination."[10] Marcus Aurelius mentioned a similar notion when he was writing to himself in what became known to posterity as *Meditations*.

"If anyone can refute me – show me I'm making a mistake or looking at things from the wrong perspective – I'll gladly change. It's the truth I'm after, and the truth never harmed anyone. What harms us is to persist in self-deceit and ignorance."[11]

If the most powerful man in the known world at the time isn't above being open to changing his mind, who am I not to do the same? Ultimately, this idea is about embracing a "middle path." It is ensuring that we don't get so caught up in ourselves that we miss the truth or miss finding new paths to knowledge and solutions.

We should also look for modern solutions using modern ways of thinking. This isn't always the key. Sometimes, we should look to the ancients, who faced very similar issues issues we are facing today – just differently. Ultimately, philosophy is about learning to think clearly about yourself and the community you are trying to serve.

All those things can be applied by an HR practitioner, a professional in any setting, or anyone for any reason! At the end of the day, do what is **right**. I think. I HR. Therefore, I know. Basically, I think. I HR. I do the right thing. It's a simple, and hopefully effective, way to describe what I believe a "Philosopher Manager" (or an HR Philosopher) to be.

I subscribe to Ryan Holiday's newsletter the *Daily Stoic*, which sends an email with thought-provoking wisdom. One email was titled, "There's Nothing Special About Philosophers."[12] It hit home as it made the point that true philosophers are regular, everyday people. They look for ways to get better every day, even if it's only a little bit. A little bit over time adds up to a lot!

One doesn't have to subscribe to Stoicism as a philosophy to understand this as a powerful concept. Philosophers aren't special. They're everyday people (to turn a phrase from Steve Browne).[13]

This is a powerful thought because **YOU** can always engage in the one thing that separates us from the rest of nature. What is that **one** thing that separates us from the rest of nature? Well, our ability to use reason and to think on a higher plane. Applying this approach to our everyday life is liberating. It means, we always have the ability to think about and choose our direction. We can choose to ignore things we can't control. We can choose our mindset. We can choose our response.

Ultimately, philosophy is about becoming a better person, and as a consequence, a better professional. "All else is simply the critique of words by way of other words," as Friedrich Nietzsche said. Marcus Aurelius would have likely concurred: "No role is so well suited to philosophy as the one you happen to be in right now."

Notes

1. CMI Insights, "The skills that employers want in the modern workplace," CMI, September 28, 2021, https://www.managers.org.uk/knowledge-and-insights/article/the-skills-that-employers-want-in-the-modern-workplace/; "6 Employability Skills for the Modern Workplace," Study in the USA, August 30, 2022, https://www.studyusa.com/en/a/2050/6-important-skills-that-will-up-your-employability; https://www.bcg.com/publications/2020/leadership-agile-blindspot; https://hbr.org/2022/04/6-strategies-to-upskill-your-workforce.

2. @rebelEducator, October 30, 2022, https://twitter.com/rebelEducator/status/1586788648799854593.

3. Moldoveanu, Mihnea; Frey, Kevin; and Moritz, Bob, "4 Ways to Bridge the Global Skills Gap," Harvard Business Review, March 18, 2022, https://hbr.org/2022/03/4-ways-to-bridge-the-global-skills-gap.

4. Timmes, Michael, "Frontline Managers Are The Lynchpins To Business Success" Forbes, October 26, 2021, https://www.forbes.com/sites/forbescoachescouncil/2021/10/26/frontline-managers-are-the-lynchpins-to-business-

success/?sh=7ec105522ebe.

5. Epictetus (author), Sharon Labell (Translator), The Art of Living: The Classical Manual on Virtue, Happiness, and Effectiveness, (New York: MJF Books, 1995), p.78

6. Epictetus, The Art of Living, pg. 79.

7. Image Source : https://www.studiobinder.com/blog/platos-allegory-of-the-cave/

8. Plato (author), Desmond Lee (Translator), The Republic, (Penguin Classics, 2007).

9. "The Highest Good: An Introduction To The 4 Stoic Virtues," The Daily Stoic, November 22, 202, https://dailystoic.com/4-stoic-virtues/.

10. Lee Shannon, Be Water, My Friend: The Teachings of Bruce Lee, (New York: Flatiron Books, 2020), pg. 8

11. Marcus Aurelius (author), Gregory Hayes (translator), Meditations, (New York: Modern Library, 2002), pgs. 73-74

12. "There's Nothing Special About Philosophers," The Daily Stoic, November 22, 2022, https://dailystoic.com/theres-nothing-special-about-philosophers/.

13. Browne, Steve, Everyday People, November 22, 2022, https://www.sbrownehr.com/.

Paul LaLonde

Paul A. LaLonde is a deliberate HR professional who believes philosophy is a difference-making pursuit in life as well as in business. Learning, teaching, and being of service to others are his purpose. Currently, Paul serves as the V.P. of People & Culture for CEDA of Cook County, Inc. in Chicago, serves as an adjunct professor at Joliet Junior College, and manages his consulting and coaching business, HR Logic. Paul is an alumnus of the SHRM National Blog Squad, named to Social Micole's Most Inclusive HR Influencer List™ in 2020 and 2021, a recipient of the 2021 HR Unite! Community Award, and recipient of a 2021 Human Resources Today MVP Award for his blog HR Philosopher. He is a proud husband, father, disobedient cat owner, Star Wars nerd, and metalhead. Connect with him on LinkedIn and Twitter at @HRPaul49.

Connect with Paul LaLonde:

https://www.linkedin.com/in/paullalondeshrmcp/

http://www.gohrlogic.com/

http://www.hrphilosopher.com/

3.

Why Women?

Your Best Workplace for the Future

Andrea Bjorkman | CEO and Co-Founder of Fizz Enterprises

I have spent more than thirty years in the corporate world as a white female and moved up the ranks at several companies to reach the executive level. For most of my career, I was a working mother of four daughters and can certainly speak to the trials and tribulations of working in a man's world and the impact past decisions had on me, other employees, and companies as a whole. The word 'culture' was not used back then but companies still made decisions, maybe unknowingly, on what they do and how they do it. And those decisions came together to create the employee and customer experience.

That employee experience, especially how it relates to women, has been a passion of mine for the last fifteen years. My goal has been about improving organizations' employee experience which ultimately should lead to the organization's overall success.

I believe solving any problem starts with educating yourself and others, especially decision-makers. That is my purpose in writing this chapter. My intention is to educate, convince, and provide assistance to leaders to help them be more successful. We all need to be a part of the solution, right?

Let's get started with a history lesson.

During both World Wars, especially WWII, women kept the factories and shipyards running by producing munitions and war supplies, all while taking care of their families at home alone. They were called upon to fill these jobs because their fathers, brothers, husbands, and sons were fighting these terrible wars overseas. "Rosie the Riveter" was born as a propaganda campaign to encourage women to fill these very important positions that were traditionally held by men. Yet, when these men returned, women went back to their low-paying, female-oriented jobs or back to working in their homes. Rosie became "Rosie the Housewife" in a reverse propaganda campaign to get back to "normalcy."

Despite the change in what was considered "normal" over the decades, women in the workforce today have not yet achieved gender parity in position or pay. Since the COVID-19 pandemic, women have lost all of the ground they had gained in previous decades. If something is not done now, one estimation suggests that it could take as long as 271 years to close that gender gap.[1]

To ground you in some facts, here are some statistics regarding women in the workforce over the last several years:

- 56.2% of women in the US are part of the workforce compared to 67.7% for men.
- The number of women in the C-Suite and senior vice-president roles have grown 17-21% and 23-28% respectively; however, women of color are severely underrepresented at only 3%.
- The pandemic caused historically high levels of unemployment for women, especially women-of-color. Eight million women-of-color were left looking for work.
- There was a huge disparity between the participation of men and women in the workforce before the pandemic; after the pandemic it only became worse with men's participation at 74% and women at 47%.
- 60% of working women would earn more than men if paid for the same working hours and education level.
- There is a huge racial disparity among unemployed women – Black women at 9.2%, Hispanic women at 9%, and Caucasian women at 6.5%.[2]

Working Mothers – Burnout is Real!

- 72.3% of working women have children under the age of 18.
- 41% are the primary, or only, earning family members, meaning they make more than their spouse. An additional 23% are considered co-breadwinners.
- Of the 35 million working mothers in the U.S., 9.8 million suffer from workplace burnout and they are 28% more likely to face burnout than their male counterparts.
- 43% of working mothers leave their jobs during the first year after their baby is born. This is a pre-pandemic number and there is no doubt that number has increased.

And then the pandemic hit. What was your experience? How did it affect you both personally and professionally? How did it affect your organization? Have you made the necessary changes to your culture and employee experience?

The Pandemic Effects – The Great Breakup[3]

The pandemic has greatly changed the lives of all of us but most notably, working women. According to an analysis of the latest U.S. Bureau of Labor Statistics report by the National Women's Law Center, men have completely recouped their job losses, while women did not and still have not.[4] In fact, 1.1 million women left the labor force from February 2020 to January 2022, accounting for 63% of all jobs lost.

While women gained 188,000 jobs available in the workforce by January 2022, they are still short by more than 1.8 million jobs lost since February 2020. It would take women nearly ten months of growth at January's level to regain the jobs they lost, the NWLC report indicated.

Why is this true? Is it only because of the pandemic?

A McKinsey report found that the pandemic worsened this development: women with children were significantly more likely than men with children to leave their jobs in 2020. That year, 1 in 4 women considered leaving the workforce or downshifting their career, versus 1 in 5 men.[5]

Women, historically, have been the family member who covers most of the childcare duties. The same is true when it comes to providing elder care.

According to Deb Boelkes, award-winning author of *Women on Top: What's Keeping You from Executive Leadership,*

> *"In many families, the lowest-wage-earning spouse chose to voluntarily resign to care for their at-home children or other family members. Many women found juggling business responsibilities with homeschooling, child care, and elder care wasn't*

worth the effort or the income to justify staying in the job."

Discrimination Plays an Even Bigger Role for Women of Color

Although I have led and been involved with many initiatives for women of color, as a white woman, I can't begin to truly know what they experience. Their lack of advancement opportunities and the ultimate negative effects to organizations is incredibly disheartening to me. The NWLC report also showed how much higher the unemployment rates are among women-of-color and disabled women.[6] In January 2022, 3.6% of all women were jobless; nearly 5% were Latinas and nearly 6% were Black women. Women with disabilities were most affected, as nearly 8% were jobless.

Unemployment rates do not include people who left the labor force entirely and are no longer looking for work. Had those individuals been included, about 5% of all women, 5.4% of Latinas and 7.3% of Black women would be considered unemployed, per the NWLC report.

Emily Martin, Vice President for education and workplace justice at NWLC, believes discrimination contributes to high jobless rates among minority women.

"Women of color face more obstacles in job seeking due to conscious and unconscious bias," she said. "They are also more likely to be single parents, and the pandemic makes it harder to find caregiving, which affects their employment."

As a white woman, it is extremely important to explicitly acknowledge my own biases.

Why Women? What Value Do They Bring?

With this very important groundwork laid, it's now time to answer these imperative questions:

- Why women?
- What is the value they bring to organizations and the U.S. economy?[7]

Organizational Value:

Quite a bit of research has uncovered that women in the workplace and gender diversity are keys to a company's financial performance:

- Fortune 500 companies with the highest representation of women on boards financially outperform companies with the lowest representation of women on boards.
- Gender-diverse teams have higher sales and profits

compared to male-dominated teams.

- A recent Gallup study found that gender-diverse business units have higher average revenue than less diverse business units.[8]

In addition, and just as importantly, women and the diversity they bring make an organization a better place to work for both men and women.

The results of the Center for Creative Leadership's research showed that having a higher percentage of women in the workplace predicted:

- More job satisfaction
- More organizational dedication
- More meaningful work
- Less burnout[9]

This research also demonstrated that having more women in the workplace was positively related to employee engagement and retention. Specifically, when asked why they stay with their current employer, people from organizations with a high percentage of women were more likely to cite positive and meaningful organizational culture, including having:

- Enjoyable work
- A job that fits well with other areas of their life
- Opportunities to make a difference

These new findings persist, regardless of participants' age, industry, organization size, leadership level, ethnicity, *and gender*.

In fact, their findings were even stronger for men on some measures. Specifically, men reported being more satisfied with their job, enjoying their work more, and not feeling as burned out if they worked for companies that employed higher percentages of women.

If these findings are not enough to convince you of the value women and diversity can bring to your organization, here are a few more:

- Female bosses are more supportive of career development.
- Female managers are more likely to aid employees with their development goals.
- Women leaders tend to be more likely to use effective leadership styles.

Additional research from many other sources shows that:

- Women have earned more bachelor's degrees than men since 1982, more master's degrees than men since 1987, and more doctorate degrees than men since 2006.[10]
- Women have a key advantage over men in soft skills, also known as emotional intelligence. Korn Ferry found that women outperform men in eleven of twelve emotional intelligence competencies.[11] According to the Department of Labor, these soft skills are now rated

as even more important to work readiness.[12]

- Women are better at problem-solving because people who differ from one another in gender, ethnicity, or other identities bring a range of perspectives to an organization; this enhances creativity and encourages the search for novel information. This, in turn, leads to better decision-making, and ultimately, greater success.

- Women are better at building trust. According to Pew Research Center's Women and Leadership survey, 34% of American workers say that women have an edge over men when it comes to being honest and ethical. While just 3% believe men are better at being honest and ethical.[13]

United States Economic Value:

Because of women's increasing labor force participation since 1970, they have added $2 trillion to the US economy. However, 63% of that progress was erased, or $1.26 trillion, because of the pandemic. It is vital to our economy to get back to that place of profit as a nation![14]

If we do not, we – as a collective workforce – will continue to lose out. The US could boost its gross domestic product (GDP) by about $650 billion per year by adding 4.85 million more women (aged 25-54) to its workforce. This would reach a level proportional to women's labor-force participation in Canada, Germany, and the United Kingdom.[15]

The value of women is clear. Now how do you attract them?

What Do Women Want?[16]

They want a job that fits well with other areas of their life, followed by enjoying the work that they do, and believing that their job allows them to make a difference in their community and the world. Many women want to have personally meaningful work that connects to their personal values, their purpose, and work-life balance. This could otherwise be known as "a calling."

Women want flexibility above all else. This flexibility relates to where, when, and how they work. Working from home is a high priority because of their propensity to be the caregivers in their families.

They want real leadership opportunities which require parity in the expectations of both men and women and the same amount of funding, supervisor support, and team size. More women leaders should be imperative for each and every company!

So, Now What?

The facts are in, the research has been shared, and your questions are answered. Now what?

For your company to achieve both the financial and workplace value that women bring to your organization, you must focus on doing all that you can to attract, promote, and retain women. The really good news is that so many of these necessary tactics will also benefit men.

Whether you are looking at attracting, promoting, or retaining women, you must provide high-quality programs and policies that are continually evaluated to assess whether benefits are equitable. Also, it's essential to identify areas where certain groups may need more targeted support.

The single most important thing you can do is to admonish sexism and offer gender parity in pay, experiences, and opportunities for success.

Attract

1. Start by reviewing job descriptions and interview processes to make sure your recruiters and hiring managers are not practicing implicitly biased behaviors.
2. Provide conscious and unconscious bias training to them all.
3. Work with companies such as Textio and Gap Jumpers to help with the best words to use and create "blind" job

applications.

4. View gaps in employment more positively.
5. Provide coaching services for rejected applicants.

Promote

1. Above all, feed your leadership pipeline with an intentional succession planning program that includes:

   - A focus on women by first identifying where the largest promotion gaps are.
   - Valuable leadership experiences that include challenging assignments. Track and provide resources and support for these assignments.
   - And include metrics such as rates of promotion for men and women, outcomes that are equitable, and look out for biased aspects of your evaluation processes.

2. Equalize the level of sponsorship, recognition, and standards for both women and men.
3. Offer special programs for women-of-color.

Retain

1. Create well-designed work-family policies such as equal scheduling and paid family leave.
2. Invest in women **now** so that it is easier to include more women at your company and on your team down the

road. Allowing senior team members who are women to leave, causes younger women to do the same.

3. Reduce burnout by:

   - Encouraging/incentivizing workers to take their allotted annual vacation days.
   - Offering "no meeting" or "refresh" days.
   - Conduct "happiness-level checks" daily as a burnout warning indicator along with the use of paid sick time, leave, etc.
   - Offer job-crafting to allow individual employees to design their jobs.

4. Double down on goal setting and accountability.
5. Build a culture of trust and safety.

Benefits:

In addition to the tactics above, you should review all of your benefits to make sure they are equitable and meet the objectives of attracting, promoting, and retaining women. They should all be prioritized towards well-being and preventing turnover. Remember, many of these benefits will appeal to men, as well.

Benefits to consider include:

- Financial education services.
- Various health and wellness benefits for both the

employee and her family such as mental health and breathing or meditation services.

- A parental leave program that allows women *and* men to share paid time off if they choose.
- Paid mental health time off.
- Coaching services for the many transitions women go through such as menopause, caring for elderly parents, empty-nesting, widowhood, etc.
- Childcare options, such as dollars towards those costs similar to tuition reimbursement, onsite childcare, emergency childcare, etc. Consider elderly options, as well.
- Create company-wide giving opportunities to women's organizations.
- Encourage employees to volunteer to help women in your community.
- Become politically active at the company and/or employee level to change policies affecting women and their families.

The time is **now** to make the necessary changes in your organization to attract, promote, and retain women. Women are demanding more from their work life and are leaving in unprecedented numbers and unprecedented rates. They no longer have any hesitation to switch jobs for better work-life balance or to leave the corporate world completely.

The number of women-owned businesses grew by 21% from 2014-2019 and women of color-owned businesses doubled by 43% . The majority of these women are absolutely in love with their jobs compared to 9% of women who say they are happy working for someone else.[17] Can you afford to lose these valuable women?

Notes

1. Dimovski, Aleksandar. "30 Powerful Women in the Workforce Statistics for 2022." GoRemotely, Goremotely, 13 Jan. 2022, https://goremotely.net/blog/women-in-the-workforce/.

2. Dimovski, Aleksandar. "30 Powerful Women in the Workforce Statistics for 2022." GoRemotely, Goremotely, 13 Jan. 2022, https://goremotely.net/blog/women-in-the-workforce/.

3. Gonzales, Matt. "Nearly 2 Million Fewer Women in Labor Force." SHRM, SHRM, 7 July 2022, https://www.shrm.org/resourcesandtools/hr-topics/behavioral-competencies/global-and-cultural-effectiveness/pages/over-1-million-fewer-women-in-labor-force.aspx.

4. "The Wage Gap Robs Women of Economic Security as the Harsh Impact of COVID-19 Continues." National Women's Law Center, 9 Mar. 2022, https://nwlc.org/resource/the-wage-gap-robs-women-of-economic-security-as-the-harsh-impact-of-covid-19-continues/.

5. "Seven Charts That Show Covid-19's Impact on Women's Employment." McKinsey & Company, McKinsey & Company, 28 Feb. 2022, https://www.mckinsey.com/featured-insights/diversity-and-inclusion/seven-charts-that-show-covid-19s-impact-on-womens-employment.

6. "The Wage Gap Robs Women of Economic Security as the Harsh Impact of COVID-19 Continues." National Women's Law Center, 9 Mar. 2022, https://nwlc.org/resource/the-wage-gap-robs-women-of-economic-security-as-the-harsh-impact-of-covid-19-continues/.

7. Clerkin, Cathleen. "'What Women Want- And Why You Want Women- In The Workplace.'" Center For Creative Leadership,

17 July 2022.

8. Badal, Sangeeta Bharadwaj. "The Business Benefits of Gender Diversity." Gallup.com, Gallup, 14 Nov. 2022, https://www.gallup.com/workplace/236543/business-benefits-gender-diversity.aspx.

9. Clerkin, Cathleen. "'What Women Want- And Why You Want Women- In The Workplace.'" Center For Creative Leadership, 17 July 2022.

10. "Digest of Education Statistics, 2021." National Center for Education Statistics (NCES) Home Page, a Part of the U.S. Department of Education, 2021, https://nces.ed.gov/programs/digest/d21/tables/dt21_318.10.asp.

11. Creator, and Kornferry. "New Research Shows Women Are Better at Using Soft Skills Crucial for Effective Leadership and Superior Business Performance, Finds Korn Ferry." Korn Ferry, Kornferry, 4 Mar. 2016, https://www.kornferry.com/about-us/press/new-research-shows-women-are-better-at-using-soft-skills-crucial-for-effective-leadership.

12. "Soft Skills: The Competitive Edge." United States Department of Labor, https://www.dol.gov/agencies/odep/publications/fact-sheets/soft-skills-the-competitive-edge.

13. Author, No. "Women and Leadership." Pew Research Center's Social & Demographic Trends Project, Pew Research Center, 7 Aug. 2020, https://www.pewresearch.org/social-trends/2015/01/14/women-and-leadership/.

14. Roy, Katica. "Commentary: More than a Million Women Have Left the Workforce. the Fed Needs to Consider Them as It Defines 'Full Employment'." Fortune, Fortune, 6 Sept. 2022, https://fortune.com/2022/09/06/women-workforce-fed-rates-consider-full-employment-katica-roy/.

15. "Resources." National Partnership for Women & Families, July 2021, https://www.nationalpartnership.org/our-work/resources/.

16. Clerkin, Cathleen. "'What Women Want- And Why You Want Women- In The Workplace.'" Center For Creative Leadership, 17 July 2022.

17. Dimovski, Aleksandar. "30 Powerful Women in the Workforce Statistics for 2022." GoRemotely, Goremotely, 13 Jan. 2022, https://goremotely.net/blog/women-in-the-workforce/.

Andrea Bjorkman

Andrea has seen it all, or shall we say, "lived through it all." As a mother to four girls, while balancing a career in Corporate America, Andrea has experienced the highs and lows of life. With a savvy career background that demanded trust and confidentiality, Andrea is empathetic and supportive – systematically tailoring results to the individual.

Candid yet thoughtful, spirited, fun, and fiercely loyal, Andrea's bubbly personality may have started young as she grew up on Air Force bases around the U.S. and overseas, demonstrating her ability to acclimate to new people and situations. Perhaps this is why her favorite quote is, "We are not what we know, but what we are willing to learn." – Mary Catherine Bateson.

A credentialed Life Coach, Andrea has mentored and coached many over the years, helping clients see patterns in their own lives and ultimately breaking through to find their greater purpose and true story.

Andrea is a former corporate executive in the insurance and financial services sectors.

Connect with Andrea Bjorkman:

https://www.linkedin.com/in/andreabjorkmanfindyourfizz/

andrea@findyourfizz.com

4.

Top Seven Secrets to Attract and Retain Great Employees

Lee Autore | Founder Goal-Time LLC, Planogol LLC, Member of Mythical Misfits Performance Troupe, WKI Certified Coach

Why are companies experiencing attraction and retention struggles? What are the biggest issues?

The workforce has changed, but our workplaces have not.

I'm going to give you my seven secrets of attraction and retention, but first, I want to set the stage and talk about what has changed. We will finish off with my vision of how these secrets could change workplaces of the future.

Picture this:

> We're sitting in the annual board meeting, and everyone is up-in-arms about employee turnover. Great people are leaving, and our competitors are snatching potential employees from us before we get their commitment. Employees are checked out and

inefficient, and managers are frustrated and starting to give up. Everyone in the room is looking at us. You and me. $h!t.

Figuring out the solutions to these problems is critical! So, let's jump in.

What is Wrong, Today?

I have been in and around several different industries for more than twenty-five years. I watched my father work for the hopes of a pension at the end of his career. I've been chasing the 401k for decades. Others chase the dream of moving up the corporate ladder, all for the hopes of finding freedom and opportunity.

The world has changed. We used to want products that fixed our needs, entertained us, or provided us with a certain status. Around twelve years ago, people stopped working to accumulate 'stuff.' Priorities shifted to having quality products and better experiences. There is a new focus on products, services, and companies that make the world better (or at least don't make it worse) that has entered our lives.

The same thing started happening within the hearts of the people that make up the workforce. They want to make the world better, and not damage it in the process. Personal motivations of employees are brought into work.

Millennials in 2023 range from twenty-seven to forty-three years old. This is our core workforce. They are not simply the "young kids" that keep trying to shake things up. They are valuable employees and team members that are changing the ways that the mainstream workforce has operated for decades. They **ARE** the mainstream workforce. I'm not even a member of the millennial generation; yet, I have been working alongside these amazing people and learning from them.

According to a GALLUP report ("*How Millennials Want to Work and Live*")[1] our current workforce has moved their focus from:

- Paycheck → Purpose
- Job Satisfaction → Personal Development
- Wanting Bosses → Wanting Coaches
- Annual Reviews → Ongoing Conversations
- Highlighting Weaknesses → Spotlighting Strengths
- "My Job" → "My Life"

Many of us (uh..."old people") balk at these shifts. They don't work within parameters of our old (maybe even tired) tried-and-true processes and procedures. Yet, some of us have looked on at these shifts in wonder, desperately trying to figure out how we can get this for our lives, too.

Why Listen to Me?

My name is Lee Autore, and I am a mechanical-engineer-turned-businessperson. I never quite fit in with the engineers. To be truthful, I didn't fit in with the business folks, either. All my efforts over more than twenty-five years of experience focused on solving business problems using technology. I understood both the executive side and the developer/engineer side and could "translate" between them.

> *"Lee, your job is to translate geek to non-geek."* – Marc Aiello, a prior manager

I have worked every angle of the Software Development Life Cycle (SDLC). I've run my own web development business, worked and managed in the controls engineering field, and managed teams. Now, I consult on million-dollar-plus technologies, projects, and companies.

I've learned a lot about businesses, people, and adapting to change. I'd like to share my thoughts and experiences with you.

How Do We Fix It?

Simply stated: do what lifeforms on earth have been doing for billions of years. **_Evolve and adapt._**

Evolution (or adaptation) is "the adjustment of organisms to their environment in order to improve their chances at survival in that environment".[2] More clearly spoken: "You have to adapt to your surroundings to survive."

How can your business adapt? What is the competition doing? Is your leadership missing a key skill set? Is someone offering solutions that can help you fill in the blanks?

Whatever you decide, be sure to avoid "analysis paralysis." According to "What Is Analysis Paralysis," written by James Chen for Investopedia:[3]

> "Analysis paralysis" is an inability to make a decision due to overthinking a problem. An individual or group can have too much data. The result is endless wrangling over the upsides and downsides of each option, and an inability to pick one.

These problems don't simply solve themselves. They will not go away if you ignore them. Ensure that you are doing your very best at the exact skills that make people **thrive** in this new world.

- Experiment
- Evaluate
- Keep the good, ditch the bad
- Repeat

The Seven Secrets

All of these secrets build on each other and each one offers a new way of thinking and action items. They could carry you from basics to being employment thought-leaders in your industry.

Let's set a very important concept. I want us to employ and cultivate **Heroes**. These secrets help you to do just that. They change the mindset.

Heroes come in all sizes from contractors to employees to team leads to supervisors, and even up to managers and executive leadership.

We just need to treat each hero at every different level that way.

Secret #1: Give your *heroes* purpose.

> When was the last time we – as a company – reviewed our mission, purpose, and vision? Are these relevant and meaningful reasons for doing what we do? Does it include a brand promise? Is this brand promise something measurable?
>
> Do our **heroes** know and understand them?
>
> Are our **heroes** onboard with the mission, purpose, and vision? Are they satisfied and excited to be following the mission? Proud of the work we are doing? Do they have changes to suggest making them better?

Do we talk about all of these elements with current **_heroes_**? Potential **_heroes_**? Managers? How can we do better?

Go to your team and ask these questions. Work on any issues you may discover from these conversations. Ensure that your company's purpose is one that will encourage and inspire your **_heroes_** to come into work and do amazing things.

Secret #2: Encourage _heroes_' personal and professional development.

What are we doing to help our **_heroes_** to grow? Are we giving them ways to learn new skills and take on new responsibilities?

Do we provide and encourage amazing mentorships within the organization? Outside of our organization? Are mentorships random? Are we carefully "matching" **_heroes_** to someone within the company who they can benefit from and help them reach their aspirations?

Have we asked our **_heroes_** what they hope to get out of working for us?

Secret #3: Become a _hero_ coach.

According to the International Olympic Committee, "a good coach is positive, enthusiastic, supportive, trusting, focused, goal-oriented, knowledgeable, observant, respectful, patient, and a clear communicator."[4]

The same "Qualities of a Great Sports Coach" PDF[5] mentions ten key qualities:

- "Understands the [Work] and Leads by Example"
- "Sponge for Knowledge, Profound Thinker, Visionary"
- "Shares the Knowledge, Educates Others"
- "Highly Energized and a Motivator"
- "Knows the [Hero], Values and Respects that Relationship"
- "Is an Effective Communicator and Teacher"
- "Is a good listener"
- "Is Disciplined, Strong in Character and Integrity"
- "Leads by Example with Very High Attitude to Hard Work"
- "Displays Commitment and Clear Passion for the [Work]"

Who are the amazing coaches you can think of? Is it Phil from Disney's *Hercules*? Mr. Miyagi from *The Karate Kid*? Paulie Pennino from *Rocky*? Ben Whittaker from *The Intern*? Coach Ted Lasso from Apple TV's show *Ted Lasso*? Was it a high school sports coach, coworker, or boss? Crazy uncle? Family friend?

One of my **heroes** is my high school computer programming teacher, Mr. Bob Conley. He really nailed every quality from the list above. Most importantly, he taught me to believe in myself.

How do you measure up to your ideal coach? Are you

being a coach to the **_heroes_** that are working under you? Take those qualities and try to exemplify them!

Secret #4: Engage your _heroes_ in real and regular conversation.

Most traditional companies have a "Suggestions" box. But who really uses them? Why do people use them? Why do people choose not to? How do they fail?

Think about periodic surveys distributed within a company that are used to find out how the company is performing. Use a combination of anonymous and identified surveys to find out how employee and manager **_heroes_** think and feel.

Consider monthly **_Hero_** Catchup meetings as a framework to allow an employee and their manager to:

- Create a safe environment for constructive criticism and accountability
- Listen and understand each other
- Discuss and celebrate strengths
- Ideate solutions to resolve company, management, and employee issues

Executive leadership tries to solve our problems using about five brains. Ones that might not be involved in the problems. Can we communicate to our heroes why the organization needs improvement? If we can, then we have greater potential for hundreds of involved and idea-sparking brains working on amazing solutions.

Frequent conversations promote engaged connection within our workforce. They encourage knowledge accumulation.

Secret #5: Help your _heroes_ change their focus from weaknesses to strengths.

All **_heroes_** have weaknesses, and most of us know what they are. What if you could have an open conversation and ask for help to develop strengths in those deficit areas? How would that feel, compared to an annual review where we focus on the weaknesses?

Some of us (at every level) don't know our weaknesses and may need help. We need to be open to suggestions, constructive criticisms, and help. Do you have a weakness? Of course. We all do. What are they? Are you able to identify them? Go talk it out and work with other **_heroes_** to evaluate and progress. Weaknesses are not a weakness or an issue/ problem...they are simply things to improve upon.

The real trick? Focus on strengths! Don't try to help someone **_overcome_** a weakness. Help them to **_build_** a strength that will **_solve_** the weakness.

Secret #6: Support and empathize with aspects of your _heroes'_ personal life.

Heroes want to use their life to do amazing things for the world **_through_** their work. Value their strengths and contributions as much as possible. Efforts of recognition can't always be this focused, but more is better; and some recognition is certainly better than none.

This secret is about work-life balance. The growing workforce wants to "work to live" rather than "living to work" now. Millennials watched their elders save every penny for forty years so they could finally "live." Then, when it came time for retirement, they were too tired, too sick, or died too early to benefit or reap the rewards of their decades of hard work.

What if we truly took advantage of our **heroes'** strengths and let them do what they do best every day? Obviously, we can't do that **all** the time, but, spread this idea across an organization and see how people flourish! We will see happier **heroes**, decreased overtime hours, less burnout, and more productivity.

Morale is our focus here. Engaging in the personal lives of our **heroes** will also increase morale. Have a hero who is a talented artist? Hang their art in the lunchroom. Performer? Hire them for an event. Does a **hero** have an anniversary, birthday, kid's graduation, or new baby? Help cheer them on and celebrate with them. If our **heroes** have personal accomplishments we don't know about, something is missing.

Secret #7: **Help your _heroes_ achieve their _dreams and goals_**.

The key message I want us all to understand is this:

Create meaningful work and an environment in which a **_hero_** can thrive. Assist them in the accomplishment of their personal dreams and goals.

These factors will cement your relationships with your **_heroes_**.

Think of a past job that you left. What if that company treated you as described above? What if they helped you start a business, coached you through buying your first home, talked through romantic and other relationship dilemmas? They would be setting you up for your future successes, right?

Would you have:

- invested more of yourself within the company?
- recruited others to apply?
- given your best efforts?
- been prouder and more excited to talk about work (more gasps, less groans)?

My Vision for the Future

I love the McKinsey Quarterly article, " *'Great Attrition' or 'Great Attraction'? The choice is yours.*"[6] It illustrates some cornerstones of my thoughts. This article describes changes in employment since the beginning of the COVID pandemic:

"... many companies are jumping to well-intentioned quick fixes that fall flat: for example, they're bumping up pay or financial perks, like offering 'thank you' bonuses without making any effort to strengthen the relational ties people have with their colleagues and their employers. The result? Rather than sensing appreciation, employees sense a transaction. This transactional relationship reminds them that their real needs aren't being met."

"... employees crave investment in the human aspects of work. Employees are tired, and many are grieving. They want a renewed and revised sense of purpose in their work. They want social and interpersonal connections with their colleagues and managers. They want to feel a sense of shared identity. Yes, they want pay, benefits, and perks, but more than that they want to feel valued by their organizations and managers. They want meaningful – though not necessarily in-person – interactions, not just transactions."

Kicking Off the Future

In our minds, let's pretend that we run a company.

We're going to rock the foundations of our company's culture. We've hired a consulting company to perform interviews of **heroes** of all levels. How do our internal **heroes** understand our brand, including our purpose, brand promise, and value statement?

We discover that no one is happy with the statements. In fact, most **heroes** don't know the statement. Those who do remember it seem hesitant and/or ashamed to say the words out loud. Why is that?

Heroes from our team speak about experiences with our clients, the ones that make them proud of the work they do.

We develop new branding. We focus on the meaning we can put into the world for our clients and our **heroes**.

Mission: *"To consult with and enable success in world-improving businesses through excellence in thought-leadership."*

We introduce every management **hero** to a new platform and train them how to use it. The platform is an online life management solution targeting life area balance. It focuses on users finding and maintaining balance by achieving dreams and goals. The platform encourages the sharing of dreams and goals between all levels of the **heroes**. It recommends that everyone work with accountability partners. We engage with the platform to provide paid access to all our **heroes** and their families.

We train all levels of **heroes** and teach them how to engage in the behaviors in this chapter. They meet with their teams' **heroes** on a regular basis and share dreams and goals.

It is obvious that we can't spend too much of our time

working on these non-billable efforts. Just one hour per month with each manager's directly reporting **_heroes_** would drive real, tangible change.

How the World Changes

Jennifer is a vice president. Nathan reports to Jennifer. She shares a conversation in which Nathan tells her he wants to start a business. They work out a plan for him to shadow her related work. They create a three-year-plan to help Nathan launch his business. Jennifer then schedules monthly meetings for him and company leaders. They agree to provide insight and advice for Nathan's new start-up.

Dreams and needs are discovered throughout our organization. Some needs involve giving a few extra minutes per week to help provide mentorship. Sometimes **_heroes_** consult on other **_heroes_**' finances. Sometimes they connect **_heroes_** to other resources that may be of help.

The real benefits are evident months later. More heroes speak up with ideas during meetings. Efficiency rises, high-cost hours decline. Managers need less resources to accomplish the same work. Profit margins increase.

Our creative talent tackles once-impossible pipedreams. Ideas come to life. Client satisfaction scores are rising. Account executives start pitching projects that help their clients succeed in new ways and change the world.

What happens as a result? Turnover decreases by an unheard-of 15%. Managers are praising human resources. Leadership recognizes the caliber of new talent coming into the building.

What Can We Do?

Earlier, I asked you to go into your minds and imagine with me. Now, we must step back.

<u>Business Owner, Founder, Advisor:</u>

- Could you see this example in your company?
- Can you feel the tingle of excitement at the potential?
- Which parts of our tale do you want to come to life?
- What can you do, tomorrow, to initiate change?

<u>Executive Leader, Manager, Supervisor, Team Lead:</u>

- Is anyone on your team a part of the "Quit and Stay Syndrome"? Checked out, but still sitting at their desk?
- Do you know anything about the dreams and goals of your **_heroes_**?
- Can you start asking questions to the right people, to present change?
- How much do you know about your **_heroes_**' lives outside of work?

<u>Employees, Interns, Contractors, and Everyone Else:</u>

- Ever thought about leaving? Tell someone why.
- Is there a "connection" to leadership that you can bring these ideas to?
- Can you initiate changes without managerial backing?
  - Vision boards
  - After-hours dream-and goal-setting brainstorms
  - Small workshops during lunch
- Do you want to work for "our" company described above?
- Are you willing to risk standing up to present change?

Act!

Now I encourage you to take a step back and go do something based on what you have learned from this chapter. These could be small steps or it could be foundation-shaking change.

I hope that I've gotten your attention and started the gears spinning in your head. I would love to hear your thoughts. Let me know if there's a leader somewhere who could use a copy of this book!

Whatever chapter from this book creates that itch in your mind...the one you can't ignore that calls to you to do something about it, and that wants you to stand up and shout something to the world...

ACT ON IT.

And then tell us what happened. This is what we live for!

Is yours a Supercompany (company version of a Superhero) that already does it all? Time for the bonus points! Look up and work towards being a "B-Corporation." That should give you a challenge!

The Seven Secrets

1. Give your **_heroes_ purpose**.
2. Encourage **_heroes'_** personal and professional **development**.
3. Become a **_hero_ coach**.
4. Engage your **_heroes_** in real, regular **conversation**.
5. Help your **_heroes_ change focus** from weaknesses to strengths.
6. Support and empathize with your **_heroes'_** personal **life aspects**.
7. Help your **_heroes_** achieve their **dreams and goals**.

Notes

1. Gallup, Inc. (2016). How Millennials Want to Work and Live [The Six Big Changes Leaders Have to Make]. Retrieved from https://www.gallup.com/workplace/238073/millennials-work-live.aspx
2. National Geographic Society. (July 14, 2022). Adaptation [Resource Library / Encyclopedic Entry]. Retrieved from https://education.nationalgeographic.org/resource/adaptation

3. Chen, James. "What Is Analysis Paralysis? Definition, Risks, and How to Fix." Investopedia, Investopedia, 22 Nov. 2022, https://www.investopedia.com/terms/a/analysisparalysis.asp#:~:text=Analysis%20paralysis%20is%20an%20inability,an%20inability%20to%20pick%20one.

4. International Olympic Committee. (Date Unknown). Qualities of a Great Sports Coach [Athletes Entourage – Coaches]. Retrieved from https://olympics.com/ioc/athletes-entourage-coaches PDF Link at

5. International Olympic Committee. (Date Unknown). Qualities of a Great Sports Coach [Athletes Entourage – Coaches]. Retrieved from https://olympics.com/ioc/athletes-entourage-coaches PDF Link at

6. Smet, Aaron De, et al. "'Great Attrition' or 'Great Attraction'? the Choice Is Yours." McKinsey & Company, McKinsey & Company, 28 Mar. 2022, https://www.mckinsey.com/capabilities/people-and-organizational-performance/our-insights/great-attrition-or-great-attraction-the-choice-is-yours.

Lee Autore

Lee Autore is the founder of Goal-Time LLC and Planogol LLC, a member of Mythical Misfits Performance Troupe, and a WKI Certified Coach. He is a mechanical engineer with a Bachelor of Science from the College of Engineering at the University of Cincinnati.

He has more than ten years as a business owner and business solutions analyst. His background includes customer support, controls engineering, digital marketing, and sales. Prior management roles varied from team lead to department head. Lee has also started a 501(c)(3) non-profit focused on conservation and sustainability.

Lee started Goal-Time as a consulting business. Lee and his team evolved it into a firm that provides small business and technology support services. Goal-Time saves entrepreneurs time, money and frustration by crafting achievable paths to success. They also provide project management, specialized start-up and business planning services.

His other start-up, Planogol, evolved out of Goal-Time's original plan which included an idea for a dream and goal management system. Planogol is a Software as a Service (SaaS) life management system in the health and wellness industry. It focuses on attaining life balance through the achievement of targeted dreams and goal. Planogol is set to release their "pen and paper" workbook in early 2023, and the SaaS website during 2024. They also offer life coaching in person and via zoom meetings.

This chapter was written to fulfill these goals and he hopes to share his expertise in this book. He plans to share through a workbook, lunch-and-learns, public speaking, retreats, networking events, and a video blog.

Lee Autore has (occasionally-balanced) creative and adventure life areas. His role in Mythical Misfits Performance Troupe is a great outlet. Lee is a ballroom dancer, juggler, whip cracker, and LED/fire flow arts performer. Mythical Misfits do a very limited number of shows local to the Dayton, Ohio area. He and his wife, Coryn, are proud parents of Skye, their four-year-old little girl. They are often found on adventures including horseback riding, amusement parks, and traveling. The Autore family strives to be generous and are strong supports for friends and family. They usually have at least one extra roommate who needed a steppingstone place to live.

Lee enjoys helping entrepreneurs reach their business aspirations. Lee aspires to bring his process to individuals, couples, and families. He knows he doesn't have all the answers, and is always looking for mentors and advisors.

Connect with Lee Autore:

https://www.linkedin.com/in/leeautore/

lee@goal-time.com

http://linkedin.com/in/leeautore

https://goal-time.com

https://planogol.com

http://try.planogol.com

https://www.facebook.com/MythicalMisfitsTroupe/

c: 937-231-1732

5.

Move from Leadership to Moving Leadership

Your Goals, Your Role, Your Choice

Cheryle Hays | Founder and CEO of InPower Strategists

> *"If your actions inspire others to dream more, learn more, do more, and become more, you are a leader."* – John Quincy Adams

Years ago, my partner and I developed and facilitated a leadership program designed for frontline through middle management for a phone repair facility owned by a major US service carrier. Before the end of the first day, we uncovered a huge problem. We had envisioned an opportunity to engage, equip, and empower new leaders; however, we unearthed a corrosive culture prevalent throughout the organization. We struggled through the first cohort, and realized we caused more harm than good by providing false hope and empowerment. We knew further efforts would exacerbate the morale problem. Our solution? We needed to meet with the CEO and identify the disconnect between our curriculum goals and the CEO/ C-suite actual goals. Discovery and discussion led to CEO approval of a two-day executive workshop. The CEO and VP of HR were on board, and we were optimistic about the team's willingness to engage and learn new skills. I mean, who wouldn't see the benefit of an engaged workforce?

During the workshop, we introduced the connection between leadership and multi-faceted results and the connection between leadership, culture, and employee engagement. We soon realized that several participants had no interest in changing their leadership approach. They believed that yelling, cursing, throwing things, berating, and belittling their employees was the only way to achieve satisfactory results. You may be wondering: *"What about turnover?"* Their mentality: *"There are always new workers available..."*

Does this sound like a place you would want to work? I don't think so. I have seen firsthand what can happen when leadership fails. I have also personally experienced failed leadership, and unfortunately, I have invested in companies where leadership has negatively impacted company growth. At times when starting out on my leadership journey, I have failed my team.

Moving forward to moving leadership is a choice, and accepting being less than you can be should not be an option. **The key to good leadership is remembering that it's a worthwhile journey, not a destination.** Don't settle for being less of a leader than you should be.

This chapter introduces you to my leadership success framework and personal growth process. We will take ownership of our success by looking inward before we place blame outward. My challenge to you is to take ownership of your personal leadership journey. Take the attitude that you don't know everything, nor do everything right all the time!. Be open to growth.

Let the journey begin.

The Leadership Success FrameworkTM

The Leadership Success Framework™ and formula were developed to represent leaders' impact on teams, departments, and overall company success. This formula is part of a larger framework specifically designed to scale businesses, allowing companies to maximize sustainable growth through empowering leadership. This formula sets the stage. As you study the formula, graphic, and supporting narrative below, reflect on the opening story and identify where you believe these leaders were operating within the framework.

Formula: Leadership Success = Personal(People +Performance)[1]

Good leaders recognize that they Lead people and manage performance, processes, and procedures. Leaders *orchestrate* SUCCESS at all organizational levels, not just at the top.

PERSONAL: At a glance, this venn diagram appears very simple. Simple, yes. Simplistic, no. As you can see, the PERSONAL section at the top is the most critical. It's not the most important, but it is, however, the most critical. "Why?" you ask. Excellent question!

Have you ever worked for a bad leader? Then, you get it. As leaders, we can easily de-motivate anyone. It takes minimal forethought, insight, or effort. It focuses on reactions, not responses. We, as leaders, have a multiplier (think of a double whammy – ouch!) impact on the success or failure of ourselves, our team, and our company.

Through self-awareness, goals, and choices, we can expand our definition of success to include higher levels of departmental and company performance as well as team and self-development. The alternative is to maintain an off-balance, narrow focus. You have a choice. Grow, try, fail, learn, and try again, or continue on the road to insanity – doing the same things repeatedly and expecting different results. A fixed mindset typically drives this second choice, harming us more than helping us.[2]

Let's start by fixing the first things first. We must begin with ourselves. If we cannot lead ourselves, how can we effectively lead others? If we cannot lead others, can we help our company achieve success? How, then, have we both lowered and narrowed the definition of success?

PEOPLE: Our team is the most crucial component of this success model. The ineffective leaders in the opening story of this chapter focused solely on the performance side of the framework, sacrificing people in order to obtain minimal results. They couldn't even say they had the company's best interests at heart; the loss in productivity due to disengagement and constant turnover was incredible.

Think about this. A person, team, department, or business is your customer when:

- You need them to do their job so you can do yours.

- They need you to do your job so they can do theirs.

These two statements, considered collectively, mean that everyone, both internal and external to your organization, above, below, and adjacent to you, are your customers, and you are theirs. Each of them, to some degree, needs your leadership.

If people are so important, why wouldn't we operate mainly on the people side of The Leadership Success Formula™? When we become people pleasers, we often abdicate our role as leaders. Whether out of fear of not being liked, our own insecurities, leadership anxiety, lack of skill, or fear of failure, this abdication of our role negatively impacts our team results and company success suffers.

Don't get me wrong- I believe in consensus building, using all the brains I have and all I can borrow, and supporting my team and my boss. We, as leaders, we are responsible for making the final decision within our scope of authority. However, we should also look forward, planning for inclusive growth and anticipating potential issues, making adjustments to prevent future problems.

PERFORMANCE: Consider this area of the Leadership Success Framework™ to include the processes developed, procedures used, and the outcomes generated. It is the product your team creates at the end of the day. Through choice or lack of knowledge, many leaders feel that producing the product/service is the only goal. Others may focus more on the process and less on accomplishing the end product. Notice I don't mention quality. People put quality and effort into what they are a part of and in what they believe. Lack of employee buy-in equals minimal quality. Focusing outside the center of the framework limits results, minimizes quality and hinders success. Leaders operating here are typically viewed as micro-managers, task managers, type "A," drivers, etc.

Unfortunately, we consider many entry-level leaders as "managers.", instilling the wrong mindset from the beginning of their leadership journey. They tend to focus solely on the "performance" side of the framework. Or, because we promote without training and leadership skill implementation help, we allow them to focus so much on relationships that overall performance suffers. Both approaches are wrong, as true success is in the middle. We should develop all components _**within**_ the framework.

When in balance, we achieve LEADERSHIP SUCCESS. We leverage, support, and grow all three areas, receiving an initial triple ROI. We remove obstacles, provide resources, and smooth the way. We develop processes and procedures to help our team both produce and grow. In short, we orchestrate. The higher your position within an organization, the greater the need to develop orchestration skills and insights.

Think of the CEO as a symphony conductor: their job is to bring goal-alignment to the company, team, and individuals; much like an orchestra's conductor brings harmony through different instruments, personalities, skill sets, strengths, priorities, and so on. Your role as leader is to orchestrate success within your team by understanding how all three aspects – Personal, People, and Performance – work in harmony.

So, orchestration is required at all levels, just to differing degrees. Just a reminder, a leader's goal is not to work their team **more** but to work them **right**! Above all, leadership is synergistic and equitable and requires the leader to have the right goals and provide the right culture (More about that later). It's all about the right balance.

Section takeaways:

- Personal, People, and Performance Success starts with you.
- You are a leader, even if only of *yourself*. If you cannot lead yourself, you will only be marginally effective in leading others.
- Operate from the middle of the framework. Move away from the center and people, performance, and results suffer, costs go up, and success is minimized.

Your Role, Your Goal(s)

> *"Culture eats strategy for breakfast"* – Peter Drucker

> *"If culture eats strategy for breakfast, remember leadership supplied the fork."*– Cheryle Hays

Help Yourself

"We never act in a way that is inconsistent with the way we see ourselves," Robin Sharma, The Leader Who Had No Title.

Becoming a great leader starts internally. Your journey moves from self-awareness through self-InPowerment™ and on to empowering others. This growth process is not a one-and-done instance, but an iterative cycle. It is used for both large and small, consecutive and sequential growth and is composed of self-evaluation and decision.

A core opportunity frequently absent from growth plans is linking hard skills, such as problem-solving, negotiations, conflict resolution, etc., with purposeful team growth. Capitalizing on this opportunity, however, allows both you and your team to achieve synchronous and exponential growth.

Above all, as you understand yourself better, cut yourself some slack, but don't justify staying where you are! We all can be victims of our circumstances, of things we've done, or of things done to us. Become a victor, i.e., become who we are **_because_** of what happened and the lessons we learned. But wait, there's more! The ultimate goal? Become a leader.

Purposely understand and use your journey to help others succeed in theirs through this five step process.

1. **Self-awareness and reflection:** Leadership starts with developing high levels of self-awareness and regularly thinking about the accuracy of what you believe and what you accept as fact. Identify where your beliefs and thoughts come from. What you assume as fact may be fiction. Emotions we feel, such as a fear of failure, fear of respect, influence, etc., are strong motivators for our actions. We may assume they are fact-based, i.e., "I can't dance," when you can, even though you may not be professionally trained. What you believe is that you aren't and can't become a skilled dancer.

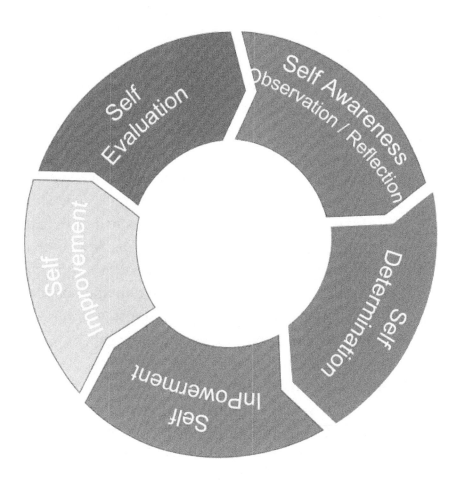

1. **Self-determination:** Now consider your strengths, weaknesses, and your goals to determine how to act; Begin by taking one small step. Self-determination is the step in the growth process where you make an ongoing pact with yourself to improve. Whenever you stumble, start again. This isn't about having "will." Struggling through based on self-will alone is frequently impossible. While willpower can't get us there, many minor decisions and small actions can. Begin believing you are *becoming* a great leader. Stop thinking, "I'd like to become a great leader." This subtle

difference is critical, as becoming requires action.

2. **Self-improvement:** Now, develop your personal growth plan. Leaders should always increase both hard and soft skills. Your plan should include areas for personal improvement, your triggers and the actions you want to take based on the leader you want to be. It includes skill improvement and how to obtain the knowledge needed, specific actions to implement this new skill, and how you will measure success. It would help to have your direct leaders' inout and buy-in, as well as that of your team, but your success is predicated on your choices and actions, not on their buy-in and support. As you develop your plan and are interested in ways to build new habits, I recommend *Atomic Habits* by James Clear.

3. **Self-InPowerment™:** My personal word, yes, but you already know the meaning! This area is where you realize the first fruits of your labor. It is your incremental gains- the fruit of your labor. You recognize the result of your progress and develop a hunger for more. You've moved from growth into growing and will challenge yourself to become more.

4. **Self-evaluation:** The full circle. Now, help others as you continue on your own personal and leadership journey. Decide on your next steps and repeat the entire cycle as needed. Over time, you value growth and lose the fear that previously held you back.

As we journey through the five S's, we become empowering

leaders. The first quote from John Quincey Adams becomes you in action.

Self-reflection Activity:

- Do you allow yourself and your team to fail forward (purposefully use failure to achieve future success) and provide safety? Or do you judge, ridicule, or compare; even if only internally? What, within you, drives those actions?
- When operating under a fixed mindset, we experience fear of failure, how others perceive us, fear of not being the best, brightest, most influential, and so on. What triggers you to react? How can you pause when you encounter that trigger and choose to respond instead?

To be truly impactful, implement the five S's throughout your leadership journey. There is always more to learn, grow, and do, so you can, in turn, become a moving leader who helps others on their journey.

Help Your Team

One of the most significant leadership roles is to help others aspire to personal greatness. So, how do you inspire, engage, equip, and empower others? The first step is knowing your role and having the right goals. As mentioned earlier, our people are the most important aspect of our success formula. Many leaders believe they are solely responsible for motivating their team. This is not possible. Believe me, as leaders we can de-motivate people. However, growth motivation comes from within, but is impacted from without.

According to Maslow's Hierarchy of Needs, we move from physiological and safety needs, i.e., the necessities of life, to self-actualization. Simply, this is the desire to become a person's best self; i.e., our growth needs. Therefore, one of our roles as leaders is to provide a culture where our team members can grow and self-motivate on their journey to self-actualization.

Create the right culture: While you cannot force people take ownership of their actions, your leadership can create a culture where those who do thrive. Your leadership and culture should positively impact team engagement, productivity, and growth. The entire team helps each other and the company while you ensure they receive equal support and reward in return. In contrast, employees unwilling to embrace their responsibility will seek another environment that is better suited for them and their needs. It doesn't mean they are bad people; they are simply a bad fit for your culture. Some on our team may need further nurturing, but some are simply unwilling to embrace needed change.

Suggested Activity: Below, I have listed values frequently seen in good cultures. The list is not comprehensive, nor should you feel obligated to use any or all of the components listed. Define your list with your team to identify your desired culture and what things look like when the value is present and when it isn't. Remember the definition of "customers" introduced above. Each person's actions impact others, whether for good or bad.

When team members feel unsafe expressing their opinions, they will not honestly participate. That's okay since it creates opportunities for your growth and change. If you encounter this opportunity for change, provide a confidential way for your team to share their true feelings, and be courageous to read/hear what they are saying. Then respond positively.

Don't be the first, second, or third person to speak during discussions! Be the last. Do not act defensively, even if something was said to make you so. That is your fixed mindset at work, and it will sabotage you. Your goal is to listen and learn. If you are sincere in your desire to foster the right culture, continue trying, and you will make progress.

Then discuss what actions to take when things break down. Actions that should be growth-oriented, not punitive.

Values Needed	How It Looks when this value is present	How it looks when this value isn't present
Trust (in you, the company, each other, and your trust in them		
Ethics		
Inclusion of styles, skills and abilities, ideas, frames of reference		
Respect offered and received from every direction		
Accountability		
Expectation		
Innovation		
Problem Solving/Critical Thinking		
Growth – value the creation of abilities		
Safety, physical and psychological		
Engagement		
Opportunity		
Innovation & Exploration		
Your Values..		

Take ownership: Take responsibility for your actions and your responsibilities. Admit when you make a mistake, and seek help when you need it. Whenever you feel defensive and want to justify your actions, follow up with a quick internal run-through of the five S's to determine where the truth is before you react. Instead, respond with your growth mindset leader.

Provide a safe environment: Honor those that contribute to the teams' success and don't take credit away from them. However, take ownership of your team's actions when things go wrong.

Allow employees to make mistakes without punishment. Allow them to grow! We learn from mistakes, not from doing something right. Encourage discovery on how to do something different in the future. Your team is no different from you. To put it bluntly, no one is perfect, so don't crucify others when an error occurs. Creating this environment helps your team own their responsibility because you are willing to own yours.

Allow team members to take responsibility for their actions: Parents know toddlers learn to walk by trying, falling, and trying again. Helping and nurturing your team is no different. They are and will become as bright as you allow them to be. Allow your team to own their professional growth, mistakes, and successes. You should provide support without removing responsibility. Support seldom means telling someone what to do and how to do it; don't micromanage. Doing this is a significant issue for most managers who feel they "know best". This means – let them do their job! Don't do it for them – you do yours! Interested to discuss what this looks like in your environment? Connect and let's talk.

How to Lead Your Team

Lead through your actions. It's not what you say; it's what you do. Yes, I know, you get it. But, let's be honest, sometimes you don't.

- **Inspire** through your example. We inspire, influence, elevate, and encourage others by being a great example. Your example is not about perfection, closed options, or closed results. Like it or not, you are a living example of your leadership, through which you open up possibilities for others.
- **Engage** by recognition and reward. By inclusion, valuing, and expecting the unique contribution of all. By allowing members to have input into issues directly impacting their roles and tasks. Don't fall prey to unconscious bias[3] and confirmation bias[4], but instead value all. You will not like everyone on your team to the same extent or the same way. Remember, "liking" has nothing to do with choosing to be a great leader for all – it's an excuse only to be an excellent leader to those that we find it is easy to lead!
- **Equip** by helping team members visualize the

connection between tasks, the value created, their role, and the company's vision. Provide the resources and support they need to be successful. Remove roadblocks.

- **Empower** by providing growth opportunities. Ask, don't tell, as much as possible, using a coaching or mentoring methodology. Allow employees to lead project or task efforts and help them identify and develop skills. Help them identify lead metrics to help prevent failure and provide safety when things get off track.

Important. Culture is the habitat in which strategy, team engagement, passion, and execution will flourish or die. Our leadership styles, choices, actions or inactions, and fixed and growth mindsets drive this culture. Don't get me wrong, your team members also impact culture. However, they will react based on what you create and allow. Culture and leadership allow your employees to engage actively and desire to produce results. *Culture is where and why the work gets done successfully.*

Help Your Company

Continue to add skills to your toolkit, such as: negotiations, conflict resolution, coaching, and mentoring. While I won't go into these in this chapter, they are frequently overlooked skills that impact company success:

Develop double vision

- <u>Zoom out.</u> Understand your company's vision and mission and how the product/service provided can fulfill both. Identify what your boss needs to be successful. Become a problem solver, not a problem creator. Identify external and internal forces that negatively impact your company's success, determine how you and your department can help, and work with leaders to innovate change.
- <u>Zoom in.</u> Help your team embrace their value and how they contribute to your company's vision and success. What other value can your team bring? What obstacles can you help eliminate? What additional skills and support does your team need? Are you protecting your team as well as protecting the company's needs?

Develop a mission

Do you have a mission and strategy for your department? Let me put it this way – are you implementing a no-strategy strategy?? Did you develop **_with_** your team or simply **_for_** your team? Your mission and strategy should provide focus and direction, and align with larger company goals. Don't forget team growth and safety. Think back to the opening story, where C-suite members put personal interests ahead of the company and the employees. Do you recognize how the "mission" of this team was single-faceted at best and how they limited future growth and overall success?

Section takeaways:

- To lead others, you must first lead yourself.
- Have multiple goals for each leadership opportunity. Include personal and team growth, restoring or maintaining relationships, allowing each person to take responsibility for their actions, along with performance and quality goals.
- Develop double vision: zoom out to understand the big picture, your company's vision, mission, strategy, and your team's contribution. Zoom in to identify and provide the leadership your team needs to achieve desired results.
- Create the right culture.
- **Inspire** through your example, **engage** by recognition and inclusion, **equip** with soft and hard skills, and **empower** through opportunities and creating a culture and environment of safety.

Your Choice – Move from Leadership to Moving Leadership

"Success doesn't choose you, you choose it." – Cheryle Hays

The ultimate goal of leadership is to make the people we interface with successful. Managers fail to become leaders when they do not embrace this philosophy. Leadership takes courage, action, determination, and prioritization. They prioritize activities that create value. How much time do you spend developing your team? Not in resolving "people" problems, but in honest development? Why settle for a narrow, limited version of success when you can accomplish so much more?

Good leaders slow things down for themselves and their team, creating calm even within the chaos. They focus on the right things, not just on doing things right.

Self-reflection activity:

The following statements will help you engage your learning mindset. Answer them honestly, with the desire to improve and grow. You aren't showing this to anyone and can't fool yourself. So, really dig deep and do a personal evaluation:

1. I choose to embrace a growth mindset by...

   ◦ I haven't because...

2. Why is this important to my team and my professional goals?
3. I choose to inspire others to...

   ◦ I sometimes fail because...

4. I choose to help others on my team develop a growth mindset by...
5. Do I sincerely want to grow as a leader?...

6. When will I have my Personal Development Plan created?...

The Unfinished Leader

"I am always doing that which I cannot do so that I may learn how to do it." – Pablo Picasso

You're traveling through another dimension; a dimension not only of sight and sound but also of mind. A journey into a wondrous land whose boundaries are that of imagination. Your next stop: the Leadership Zone! The story is yours. It's unfinished, but you are becoming an inspiring, engaging, equipping, and empowering leader. Use this acronym as a reminder of moving leadership.

Motivate

pe**O**ple through

Vision,

Inspiration

i**N**clusion and

en**G**agement

Thank you for joining me on this leadership path. Your goals, Your role, Your **CHOICE**. Want to explore your journey further, or are interested in delving deep into your personal and team leadership potential? Feel free to connect with me via LinkedIn. Just use the links in my profile.

Enjoy the journey!

Notes

1. Developed by Cheryle Hays, InPower Strategists; component in InPower Strategists Business Growth Model
2. Dweck, Carol. Mindset: Changing the Way You Think to Fulfil Your Potential. Robinson, 2017.
3. Unconscious Bias: the unsupported judgment in favor of or against one thing, person or group and against another, whether intentional or not
4. Confirmation bias: the tendency to interpret new evidence as confirmation of your existing beliefs

Cheryle Hays

Cheryle Hays is set on changing the way businesses look at leadership. As a Personal Leadership Expert, executive coach, and strategist, Cheryle helps leaders, teams, and companies maximize their potential. Her background reflects movement from her entry-level into business, through mid-level leadership and up through EVP level, spanning more than twenty-five years of leading highly productive teams, and in developing, and facilitating leadership programs for Fortune 500, large and growing companies in the DFW area. Cheryle holds an EMBA from Texas Christian University, using her business acumen to mentor small and start-up businesses since 2016.

When she's not busy helping her clients achieve success, Cheryle enjoys her role as a conference speaker, podcast guest, and guest lecturer for local universities and colleges.

She is also an angel investor, frequent judge and mentor for Texas Christian University Values & Ventures competition, Entrepreneur's Organization Global Student Entrepreneur Awards, and mentor to start-up businesses in the Fort Worth, TX area. Cheryle currently serves on the Board of Directors for Fort Worth Academy, where she continues to foster leadership, strategic thinking, and entrepreneurship for our next generation.

Cheryle is a very proud parent of two remarkable children, enjoys coffee, wine, good times with friends, and meeting new people!

Connect with Cheryle Hays:

https://www.linkedin.com/in/cherylehays/

https://calendly.com/inpower-strategists/vc

6.

Relationships

The Key to Having Advantages for Life

Ron Chambers | President of The
International Chambers Group

Business

In the early 1980's, I was a struggling musician and looking for a way to supplement my income. I went to meet my landlord (Al) to pay my rent and mentioned this to him. He always seemed interested in what I was doing which made me feel like a friend more than a tenant. It was obvious to me that he was a successful businessman but also genuinely cared about me. He said, "Why don't you come work with me?" I asked, "Doing what?" Selling real estate." I asked him how much money could be made and he replied, "As much as you want." I thought to myself, "*This man who I have previously only had a transactional relationship with is trying to help me!'"* Because of this suggestion/offer, I decided to get my real estate licenses. This involved enrolling in the forty hours of training, and reporting to his office upon obtaining these licenses and completing the training. He had a single-office company with six other realtors who had a serious focus on investment real estate. All six of the agents owned property of their own and were real estate investors as well as listing and selling homes. I learned investment real estate right out of the gate! All while listing and selling houses. If I had gone to any other company, I would not have learned the investment side of real estate. It was a great gift. I went on to be a realtor, a real estate investor, and I had a successful business. While we were working together, our relationship grew deeper. It also gave me more opportunities to give back or pour into his life. I became close with the other agents and they poured into me and my career in real estate as well. I am very grateful for the opportunity that this real estate office gave to me. I'm even more grateful that Al saw something in me that I didn't know I had.

This was my first real experience running my own business and I liked it. There was no going back now! All of this was possible because of my relationship with my landlord. He was one of the most significant mentors in my life! It was a gift, and gave me an advantage on life, for life!

When I was growing up in Detroit, I had a best friend named Tom and his dad owned a printing business with his brother. My dad worked at General Motors, and was able to provide a good home for our family with all the necessities. My best friend's dad provided a bigger, nicer home. He drove a Cadillac; my dad drove a Ford station wagon. (Remember those?) My friend's family had a cottage on a lake and a boat. They would spend all summer living there while commuting back to the city for work throughout the week. We went to visit our relatives once a year for a week when dad had his vacation. I was able to spend a lot of time at that cottage because of my relationship with my friend and his family. They were like *my* second family. I'm sure some of you had, and maybe still do have, an extended family just like this. Tom and I would go to work at his dad's printing shop on Saturday mornings, sweeping floors, cleaning the bathrooms, and taking out the trash. I would watch Tom's dad at a printing press. He once said to me, "Ya hear that, Ronnie?" I replied, "Hear what?" He said, "Another nickel, another nickel, another nickel!" Did you know printing machines can talk? He was showing me how the press was making him money! He planted the seed of business ownership at an early age. By the way, Tom and I also did other things to make money when we were kids. We had paper routes and always had money to buy model cars and other things we wanted. In case you're wondering what a paper route is...well people used to get their information in a print form before we had computers and the Internet. In Detroit, we had two newspaper companies. There was a morning edition newspaper, The Detroit Free Press and an afternoon edition newspaper, The Detroit News. These papers would pay kids to deliver their editions to people's houses, so Tom and I had paper routes with both companies. In the morning before we went to school, we would pick up *The Detroit Free Press* and deliver their papers. After school, we would pick up *The Detroit News* and deliver their papers. It was wonderful because we always had money! We were best friends, business partners, and rockin' life!

I was only ten years old when I met Tom and his family. I quickly learned the value of good relationships. I got to participate in and experience more things than my family could provide. It was a gift, and, again, an advantage on life, for life!

Let's dive a little deeper into my parents, my childhood, and background. I find it important to mention that my dad, like Tom's dad and uncle, had an entrepreneurial side as well. In fact, he had a side hustle painting houses. He would paint houses mostly in the summertime. He would canvas one of the higher-income neighborhoods to find exterior paint jobs and earn some extra money. I remember wanting to go help my dad at an early age but he made me wait until I turned sixteen. I loved working with my dad! He taught me how to paint and paint well! I would use that skill later to take his side-hustle, turn it into a full-time business, and eventually expand into a home remodeling company. That's a story for another book! When I was growing up, I had never heard the word 'entrepreneur,' so, of course I had no idea what it meant. Even though it wasn't something we discussed, my mom had the entrepreneurial bug, too! I remember the things she would do to earn extra money. She bred and sold dogs and she made ceramics and sold them. She worked at a dry cleaner's while I was at school.

My parents wanted more in life, and they worked hard but never really went "all in" on business ownership like Tom's dad did. They taught many other things like how to treat people, extend a hand to those in need, honesty, and integrity, to name a few.

It was a gift, and an advantage for life!

Mentors

Why should we have mentors? They can help you achieve more success and gain that faster. They can help you avoid costly mistakes, help you save time, alleviate or avoid frustration, and even save money in some cases. Who is mentoring you? I have mentors in different areas of my life. Some for my business, some for my personal life, some for physical and mental wellbeing, and some for my spiritual life.

I don't know if I can explain why I do this, but I have always sought out mentors and with hindsight I know they are a major factor for any success I've had. I think we are all born with the desire or need to be taught. When we were infants, someone potty-trained us, taught us how to eat with a spoon and fork, how to walk, and how to talk. Later we learn to ride a bike or skateboard, learn to play an instrument, and as teenagers, drive a car. I wasn't a very good student so I would reach out to others who excelled in Algebra or another subject I disliked or struggled with to help me, or ask the teacher for extra help. All of these examples forged lasting relationships. It's just natural and necessary to be mentored, so why do some people stop or even avoid it altogether? Is it fear? Is it pride? I believe they just stop asking for help. One of my realtor friends, and a mentor, would say: "If you don't A-S-K, you don't G-E-T."

Relationships and Your Business

Having good relationships in your business can open doors you could never open alone! I was in a training done by a highly successful B2B salesperson (Melissa Peters – LegalShield) who said prospecting for 'relationships' is a smart way to do business. A good relationship can feed your business for the rest of your life. One of my business mentors has always trained new people to ask for help. People you have created and maintained a relationship with will **want** to help you. Another one of my business associates leverages his relationships in the following way: he asks them to introduce him to their contacts. He leans on his relationship with them to start a relationship with people he doesn't know yet! This leveraging one relationship to gain another relationship approach has served him very well.

Relationship Suggestions

Seek out people you respect, share similar values with, and someone who has taken their business to the place you want yours to be. Acknowledge success, give sincere compliments, be humble, and ask for help. Volunteer at Chamber of Commerce events, non-profits, or at church. In other words: lend a hand in your community. Be a giver! You may have heard, "What goes around comes around." The Bible says it like this: "Whatever a man sows, he shall also reap." Sow good seeds, and good things will sprout and grow. Your business and your life will benefit greatly.

Last Story

You may remember me mentioning that I was a struggling musician in the early eighties. During that time, I met a man who had a sound and lighting company and his name was Tony V. The company was very good! We liked them so much that, now, my band tried to use them whenever possible. He liked us as well and also wanted to work with us. He would do everything possible to be available for our shows. We had a great relationship! Everyone who hired Tony's company liked working with him. So, what do you do when you find something, or someone, you like? Whether it is a restaurant you tried, a movie you've seen, a mechanic you've used and trust, or a sound company you work with? You tell other people about them! So, we promoted them to everyone we could. Thunder Audio went on to be one of the premier sound and lighting companies around, working with some of the biggest artists in the world and some of the biggest venues and arenas in the world. It's a great success story. My band had a small part in that story. We were willing to share Tony's skills with others knowing that someday his success would cause us to lose him. Two things to note here: Tony provided excellent services and built relationships. Those relationships, fostered by the excellent services provided by his company, powered Thunder Audio and promoted it to heights he could never have gone to without them.

Summary

We all know people do business with people they know, like, and trust. That's why networking is so effective. Your business relationships are an extension of your sales force and you of theirs. Your reputation is the best asset you have. Operate with honesty, integrity, and humility. Be responsive, be punctual, recognize the contributions of others, and be good at what you do. Be the expert. Be friendly and you'll gain and maintain friends/friendships. Most people have an innate desire to help other people, so don't be afraid to ask for help.

When you have and maintain good relationships, you can have mentorship, including valuable input and accountability. Everyone needs it to grow. Remember to ask for referrals. Your relationships are worth a fortune!

Ron Chambers

Starting in his adolescence, a mentor helped initiate Ron Chambers with the professional goal of entrepreneurship. Assisting with the start of his own business and learning the independence and development that comes from the relationships involved, Ron grew his first business along with his individual professional and work ethic. Learning every corner of business development through a detailed relationship with his mentor, Ron was able to learn the foundation of a business from the creation of his product as well as the development of consumer relationships and expanding those relationships to help build personal marketing connections. Through all the business education gained in this early mentorship, Ron was learned the value of relationships at the base of work ethics and helping proceed business development on every level.

Throughout his career, Ron Chambers has spent many years focused on the safety of his clients. This includes decades of work with LegalShield to help protect employees and employers with the benefits of Identity Theft Risk Management and much more. Beyond this benefit, Ron has worked for many years in various industries, focusing on the benefits of his clients in many ways. Often consulting business owners and management on benefits that can help improve productivity and profits, benefits for the improvement of employee culture and overall sales has been Ron's goal for many years.

Early on in his career, he made his way up the corporate ladder with various companies, offering business skills to major companies that benefit our environment among other things but always returned to his own business where he was able to work toward the benefit and professional development of his clients.

Ron has found his long-term passion and skill upon which The Chambers Group was eventually built with the use of very sturdy and reliable relationships. Ron Chambers launched The Chambers Group more than twenty years ago including the offer of LegalShield/ID Shield as a supplemental employee benefit. This grew in 2020 to include Telehealth and other essential benefits to help employers due to COVID and beyond.

The Chambers Group has always supported Associations and Chamber of Commerce, understanding the essential role they play particularly in small businesses. In 2021, the

Chambers group launched the "Chambers 4 Chambers" initiative, a "Non-Dues Revenue" program, bringing new innovative benefits to attract new members and retain current members.

With all of these benefits available to others, Ron travels throughout the state and country working with Benefits Brokers, Insurance Agents, HR Directors, and Benefits Specialists to implement the "Advantages for Life" as part of their benefit offerings. He works with business owners, companies, colleges, school districts, and municipalities to help reduce employee stress and absenteeism and increase productivity and profits. Ron also educates his clients about identity theft in the workplace including state and federal requirements, how it affects their employees, and how to protect the business and its employees. The Chambers Group has a vast network of "Trusted Advisors" and "Services Providers" to address any business need you may encounter.

Connect with Ron Chambers:

https://www.linkedin.com/in/ronchambers-chambersgroup/

7.

What's the Secret to a Successful Executive?

A More Successful Executive Assistant

Angie Dodge | CEO and Founder A Squared
Personal Consulting

"I just figured she was holding all my calls. Turns out she's been running the company."

In nearly every movie, there is a scene in which people are in a meeting, talking about something that's obviously very important. Secrecy is imperative. One of the characters – usually the chief executive or the general – declares, "clear the room," and everyone but the most trusted assistant departs.

I've always wanted to be that trusted assistant. Having been in that role for several organizations for twenty-five years, I now run my own business advocating for a more prominent, influential role for executive assistants in organizations of all kinds.

You might think that executive assistants (EAs) have all but disappeared in the current environment of flattened organizational charts, outsourcing, and working remotely. More and more, organizations are more fluidly structured, with an emphasis on fewer people doing all the heavy lifting as jacks-of-all-trades. Theoretically, this is the favored business model today. In practice, what we hear over and over are accounts about frazzled corporate leaders dealing with schedules in shambles, meetings canceled, emails not returned, and phone calls sent to voicemail and never returned.

To myself and many others, the current organizational environment is at a crucial inflection point where focus and goals expand beyond their original scope doing nothing but creating organizations filled with frustrated employees. The goal is to create an environment where focus and goals expand beyond their original scope. Time, money, and effort is wasted as frenetic employees at all levels struggle to complete tasks, fulfill important objectives, or just get on top of day-to-day functions.

Executive assistants, properly deployed and fully trusted, can help address these conditions, and save overhead costs in the process. EAs at the C-Suite level can be instrumental in achieving improved time-management, which is a critical benchmark of an organization's success.

It also might appear that current business conditions are not conducive for what I propose. There are fewer executives at the top of many corporations, for one thing. Further down the ranks, people are choosing to work from home, making it impractical to have an executive assistant; much less an administrative assistant, much less an executive assistant. There is also the looming issue of salary inequity, as most executive assistants are female.

Yet, these obstacles can be overcome. Executive assistants are critical contributors to enhancing organizational productivity and bottom-line profit growth.

Before getting into the details of executive assistant roles and responsibilities, let's look at current trends for the position:

The management website Zippia used a database of 30 million profiles, and found that:

- There are over 353,903 executive assistants currently employed in the United States.
- 86.9% of all executive assistants are women.

- The average age of an employed executive assistant is 48.
- The most common ethnicity of executive assistants is White (75.5%), followed by Hispanic or Latino (10.4%), Black or African American (7.1%) and Asian (4.6%).
- The highest demand for Executive Assistants is in New York City.
- In 2021, women in EA positions earned 98% of what men earned.
- Most EAs work in public corporations.[1]

Clearly, the market exists for ambitious individuals desiring careers in organizational environments. The title of this chapter expresses exactly what I believe, based on all of my years working with high-level executives in multiple industries. In that time, I was an executive assistant to twenty different C-Suite executives – this equates to a new boss every year and a half. Those executives were promoted, their teams hit or surpassed their goals, and their companies benefited with higher efficiency and profits.

Was I responsible for **_all_** of this success? Certainly not. I do think that I contributed a great deal to the amazing work these executives achieved. A Forbes Magazine article detailed the contributions of executive assistants this way:

> There is one position often overlooked by the most ambitious and successful entrepreneurs. No, it isn't your VP or manager. It's your executive assistant."[2]

The writer, Ryan Westwood, was referencing entrepreneurs, not your typical senior corporate executive. Yet, his observation has special relevance today. In large multinationals, Silicon Valley startups, or new high-tech ventures, everyone in an executive decision-making capacity is expected to operate with entrepreneurial instincts. Anticipate trends. Identify new products or services before they exist. Act with rational, all-deliberate speed. Hockey great Wayne Gretzky inadvertently described the creative mind this way: "Don't look for where the puck **is**. Go to where it's going to be."

Of course, this isn't everyone's strong suit. Purely from the human resource perspective, performance expectations can be all-consuming, quickly leading to burnout. It need not be this way; if the executives could count on the skills and temperament of an experienced, heady executive assistant to share the load and keep things running smoothly.

So, what are those skills? What does a modern-day executive assistant look like? What kind of person fits the mold of a modern-day EA? Here are my ABCs of executive assistant excellence:

Acceptance & Acknowledgement

The very first quality of an exceptional executive assistant is his/her mindset. The EA must understand and acknowledge that their success is a shared success with their executive and without that level of loyalty and commitment, no success will be found. The executive must embrace and accept that the relationship with the executive assistant is a **partnership**. This is non-negotiable, yet a collegial one if the executive and the assistant possess a mutual understanding of their respective roles.

A proficient executive assistant is a person who identifies needs – even those unspoken – in the business relationship. Many of the executives I have worked with were nearly slavish in their devotion to business objectives. Their focus was so intense that, in many cases, they were blind to situations that needed attention. A skilled assistant sees these problems and is often able to resolve them without having to bother the executive.

Here's an example:

> Incoming emails pile up in the inbox. The executive assistant, with the ability to access the boss's email, can decipher the important from the unimportant and therefore prioritize accordingly; this is an immense time saver. Incidentally, this can be done remotely. The same can be done with the calendar of meetings, appointments, etc.

As this example suggests, a productive working relationship between the executive and the assistant is only possible if there is a bond of trust, and an acceptance of mutual value. This is the perfect definition of an effective collaboration.

For executives and their report to work effectively, acceptance of their respective roles is fundamental. The "boss" is in charge, but the EA isn't so much a subordinate as a colleague who works in tandem.

In my experience inside highly complex organizations, too much time is often wasted on bottom-up reporting grudges and boss-subordinate rules. It's only human; we've all experienced this. However, there are ways around such obstacles.

It starts with finding common ground rules. The executive is responsible for achieving organizational goals. The executive assistant takes on everything that distracts from that objective. It may mean going for coffee. It may also mean standing in on important meetings when the executive is away, or dealing with a disgruntled manager who hasn't had a raise. In other words, the successful executive assistant serves as a trusted ally, with the ability to solve problems and overcome hurdles that prevent the executive from doing their job effectively.

I've found that one of the best management practices to avoid role confusion is to create organization charts from the top down. Once created, they are put in a drawer, only to be used as a reference; and while interacting with everyone as a partner, not a subordinate. This requires that top executives cede some responsibilities to others. It means delegating. It means having high expectations based on mutual acknowledgement of roles. Alert executive assistants in this synergy are ideally positioned to be candid, confidential advisors with clear, important duties.

A friend told me about the key role an executive assistant played in determining the outcome of a competition among three top executives vying to succeed the current CEO of a major financial institution. The competitors were **all** well-known, ambitious, and talented. The person who won out had a decisive advantage: he had a superlative executive assistant who managed the executive's organizational radar network, always tuned in to problems and opportunities in the sectors he oversaw. He relied upon his assistant to handle this duty, and his EA executed it beautifully.

> *A word of caution: it is vital that the organization accepts and acknowledges the partnership relationship of the executive and his/her assistant. In my experience, some individuals will try to get around the assistant, demanding to speak directly to the executive. Others will demean the assistant's role via various modes of communication like the rumor mill, texts, etc. On the other hand, some executives mistakenly use their assistants as gatekeepers and office security guards. These issues can be handled, or at least diffused, if the executive clearly communicates by words, actions, and appearances that the assistant is a trusted partner.*

Nothing conveys this better than including the assistant in almost all management meetings, even those tagged as confidential. When someone says, "clear the room," or "we need to speak in private," the wise executive insists that the assistant stay.

Business Partnership

Relationships among individuals are complex, ever-changing, and difficult to master. This is a matter of common sense for the vast majority.

In the organizational environment, relationships take on a specific economic and managerial aspect. People of wide backgrounds, talents, and experiences somehow must figure out how to work together and get along well with others. Cooperation and trust are essential to this process; yet – as we know from experience – values can be lost, diminished, or forgotten for any number of reasons.

To be successful, executive assistants must master the intangibles of the relationship with the person they work with. Like knowing when the person is stressed or distracted. In other words, they are adept at sensing problems that haven't fully emerged yet. Taking control of situations that are getting out of hand, such as delayed email responses, or too many meetings.

These skills **_can_** be taught; but the EA that I have in mind possesses these skills innately. This person is always alert, staying a step ahead, a day or week in advance, plugging gaps in process, suggesting alternative ways to overcome obstacles and clear the path for meeting objectives.

Let me give you an example from a colleague:

> A major food retailer with stores and manufacturing facilities had a consumer affairs function responsible for not just collecting customer feedback and complaints, but also analyzing them for trends that could have far-reaching public safety effects. The consumer affairs manager noticed a slow, but increasing, number of complaints about the company's canned green beans – they had a tinny, bitter flavor. She took the analysis to the manufacturing group, who essentially brushed away the matter as insubstantial. Next, the manager took it to the executive assistant of the CEO, who quickly alerted their boss. The very next day, the green bean production line was shut down until new procedures were implemented to ensure that the cans were tightly sealed to avoid spoilage and bacteria growth.

There are some key takeaways from this anecdote:

- The consumer affairs manager knew something needed to be done about the bad product and when they were faced with no action, they went to the person they knew would take action: the CEO's executive assistant.
- Because of the relationship that was built between the two and the EA having a reputation as a "person that gets it done" the potential problem was quickly fixed. That's how responsible management operates.

The consumer affairs manager went on to become VP of another retailer's consumer-facing operations. The executive assistant retired with a handsome package and an outpouring of heartfelt compliments from throughout the organization.

The broader lesson is that those who possess inordinate and intrinsic analytical and people-centric skills almost always, without fail, rise to the top. I believe strongly that executive assistants make up a preponderance of those who rise.

Here's more from Melba Duncan in the Harvard Business Review, talking about an executive assistant she placed with the CEO of a major insurance firm:

> "The EA fills an informal leadership role, has an unparalleled ability to read complex settings, and can respond to challenging people and circumstances."

Duncan goes on to quote the senior insurance executive with what I think is the perfect description of the accomplished executive assistant. I couldn't say it any better.

> A spectacular executive assistant can defy the laws of the physical world. She (or he) can see around corners."[3]

Collaboration

Collaboration is a much-used word in management circles, and I use it here because almost everyone knows its meaning. However, I like to think of collaboration as an **_alliance_** between and among individuals in an organizational setting.

Either word suggests a relationship built on trust and need. Nations are involved in alliances to protect and extend common goals. Nonprofit entities could hardly exist without alliances with private and public funding sources. A baseball team and a church congregation are examples of collaborative undertakings, in which people come together to achieve a common purpose; corporations and nonprofits are no different.

In the business world, collaboration among divisions, subsidiaries, and departments is essential. This is self-evident. Yet, we all know of examples in which a company fell apart due to internal conflict, opposing goals, and misunderstood objectives.

On a personal level, a collaborative endeavor(s) works best if those involved see eye-to-eye with things like titles and established authority. A collaborative endeavor(s) does not work best if used to stifle ideas and prevent constructive criticisms. Here is the nexus in which an experienced, creative, and alert executive assistant can make a huge difference.

Melba Duncan of the Harvard Business Review writes about this point:

> "Expert assistants understand the unspoken needs and characteristics of the people with whom they work. They respond to subtle cues and react with situational appropriateness. A good assistant quickly learns what an executive needs."

It begins with familiarity of the organizations' goals, strategies, vision, and purpose. The EA will quickly become familiar with their boss' areas of expertise and blind spots, so they can effectively manage both.

Continuity is something most people do not think of when thinking about the impact a great EA can have on an organization. Unless you are the EA for the CEO of the organization and get to move with them to their new role, most EAs stay in their position while a new executive takes over the corner office. What that new executive will soon learn is the best onboarding they can receive will be from their new EA. They will be able to share the lay of the land, a personal run down of their new team, as well as how to quickly and efficiently move through the organization.

This description flourishes in true collaborations.

Challenges & Opportunities

The business environment for executive assistants (EAs) is improving, according to reliable sources in the compensation field. Of course, actual salary packages for EAs vary widely by location. New York City pays the highest, followed by San Francisco – two of America's most expensive cities. According to the compensation website, Comparably.com, salaries for Executive Assistants in the US range from $25,000 to $187,654; with a median salary of $62,000. The middle 57% of Executive Assistants make between $62,000 and $103,000, with the top 86% making $187,654.

This is a vast difference from pay for assistants in the 1960's work-world of Mad Men. And it's worth noting that these numbers represent salary **only**; many top EAs are eligible for annual bonuses and stock options.

This data, I believe, underscores the argument that executive assistants are coming into their own as highly valued human resource assets for organizations large and small.

These salaries are below executive compensation at the C-Suite level. However, the gap is closing. My experience in the industry tells me that women are gaining respect and value in enlightened organizations, both public and private. Importantly, no company wants to run afoul of broader societal trends in which women play increasingly significant leadership roles throughout business and industry, the professions, and STEM fields. Employees entering today's workforce in a specific workplace are exceedingly sensitive to issues of fairness and equity. It behooves rational senior management to address these matters with focus and credibility.

Due to organizational changes, downsizing, and reorganization of businesses, the function of the EA has shifted significantly during the last five to ten years. There is no longer any need to bring in the coffee and sit at a typewriter. Those who work in this field are crucial to a company's bottom line; thus, more time, energy, and money must be put into retaining and developing the industry's professionals.

Career Goals & Advancement

Is there a viable career path for executive assistants? Yes, most definitely.

Not only are their numbers increasing in organizations nationally, EAs can begin with entry-level careers and move up the organizational ladder in the traditional, American business model. One important development is that in a downsized organization, the role of the executive assistant becomes more essential.

Not long ago, before the 2008 market crash – and well

before COVID – employees in low to mid-level positions had their own administrative assistants (a.k.a. secretaries). These EAs were tasked with any number of largely functional, and often demeaning, chores such as fetching coffee, reserving restaurant tables, typing and retyping memos, dialing phones, removing spots from neckties, getting laundry at the cleaners, etc.

Happily, these days are long gone. In many organizations I am familiar with, one EA coordinates the work of several managers simultaneously; taking on critical tasks, connecting with other EAs on common concerns, and keeping their execs tuned to the subtleties of organizational culture. This is undoubtedly good progress, but I prefer one-with-one working relationships. Top EAs are in effective, symbiotic relationships with their report; that is, they are mutually dependent in achieving business objectives.

These are career positions with advancement potential. Some corporate management consultants envision a new model in which EAs have their own career advancement channel based upon performance, compatibility, and other attributes. They are present at the Department and Division Levels, and are able to move into Senior Level and C-Suite positions with appropriately accompanying salaries and benefits.

Executive Assistants in Action

> "I always found it amazing the number of spinning plates that executive assistants manage – without really missing a beat."

That's Tammy Schaff, a previous co-worker and Director of Development of a regional nonprofit organization. Tammy learned quickly that one of the best things she could do was to partner with her boss's EA. Doing so gave her the inside track on what was happening in the department and helped make her job a bit easier when it came to scheduling time with the Executive.[4]

Maybe EAs aren't magicians; but these days they are expected to handle not just mundane chores, but also serve as a trusted sounding board, a valued advisor, and a confidant to the individual they work with.

These responsibilities are increasing. More organizations are relying upon trained, experienced executive assistants (men and women) to be the sounding boards for their management colleagues. They perform mission-critical roles with higher levels of authority and influence, always with a focus on improving overall efficiency in time management and the realization of objectives in partnership with their executives.

A great EA is resourceful, meaning they trust their gut, come up with novel ideas, know how to get the work done, and always look for ways to improve. Performing these roles is multi-faceted. The best executive assistants can read the minds of their associates. They are proficient at looking for signs of distraction, stress, or depression. They must be willing, and trusted, to speak their minds when things are going off-kilter or problems remain unresolved. EAs must create their own internal networks among colleagues to gain first-hand information about looming issues within the ranks. They must possess the confidence to speak up, suggest alternative solutions to vexing problems, and – in an overall sense – be the executive's alter ego.

The Future for Executive Assistants

A great executive assistant can positively impact all levels of an organization. That much is clear. EAs are coming into their own, according to management consultants and HR managers alike. The status of these positions (and the people who hold them) and salaries are increasing, and trust is mounting.

Beena Mathew, Regional Executive Senior VP of a top 3 financial institute, bluntly asserts that she will not take a job without having an executive assistant. Why? Because it means she is acknowledging that she's not a "do-it-all perfect," and thus requires a person with whom she can collaborate – a capable person who possesses complementary skills and temperament. Over a twenty-five-year career in banking, Mathew says always having an executive assistant has been instrumental in her success.

A great EA is an investment, not an expense. Finding that perfect fit where her EA is strong in the skills that she is not is worth its weight in gold and has been instrumental to her success. She also gives credit to her EA for being integral in her team's high level of employee engagement with the planning and facilitation of engagement events and programs.[5]

Make no mistake, there are headwinds to deal with. The COVID pandemic generated an entirely new and unplanned list of challenges to organizations of all kinds. The very notion of an iconic headquarters edifice is under review. Individuals are working remotely; and some genuinely resent having to return to the office. Supply chain dilemmas have disrupted operations of global manufacturers and consumer product makers.

Alongside these challenges, executives, Boards of Directors and Management Consultants are being forced to rethink their organizations from bottom to top.

- Who is expendable?
- Who is irreplaceable?
- What can we do without or outsource?
- Should we bring everything together in one locale?
- How do we respond to the pressure for quarterly growth and maintain a clear focus on new opportunities requiring major investments in plant, equipment, and people?
- How does a nonprofit that is strapped for cash remain relevant and sustainable?

Executive assistants will not be tasked with solving these issues. Of course not. They can and should, however, play an influential role in helping to overcome some of these obstacles by working collaboratively with their executive colleagues to navigate through the choppy waters of change.

This symbiotic relationship between executive and executive assistant is my vision and my passion; and it's one that I have nurtured for years. I began my consulting business at a time of great risk, because I believed that executive assistants are truly integral, and invaluable, to organizational success. I am even more convinced today that this is a solution that will make a defining difference in today's fast-moving and uncertain environment.

Notes

1. "Executive Assistant Demographics and Statistics [2023]: Number of Executive Assistants in the US." Executive Assistant Demographics and Statistics [2023]: Number Of Executive Assistants In The US, 9 Sept. 2022, https://www.zippia.com/executive-assistant-jobs/demographics/.
2. Westwood, Ryan. "4 Reasons Successful Entrepreneurs Need Executive Assistants", www.forbes.com, Forbes Magazine, Dec 2, 2014
3. Duncan, Melba. "The Case for Executive Assistants". www.hbr.org. May 2011. https://hbr.org/2011/05/the-case-for-executive-assistants.
4. Schaff, Tammy. Interview. Conducted by Angie Dodge. 01 Nov

2022.

5. Mathew, Beena. Interview. Conducted by Angie Dodge. 01 Nov 2022.

Angie Dodge

Angie Dodge is the CEO and Founder of A Squared Personal Consulting. She currently lives in Cincinnati, Ohio, and is a Buckeye at heart! Angie has spent her twenty-five year career as an Executive Assistant to C-Suite Level Executives in a variety of industries supporting several executives. To be more specific, Angie has supported 1.56 executives a year before starting her own company. Angie is not just a CEO and Founder, but also a chameleon that can change her spots for every executive that she has supported. One highlight of her career is winning Civilian of the Year when supporting the USAF while living in Spangdahlem, Germany.

It was this experience that led Angie down the path of becoming an entrepreneur and founding A Squared Personal Consulting. She has taken her years of learning from top executives and made it her mission to help other executives and business owners grow and succeed by providing executive level support for all their administrative needs.

Although entrepreneurship came later in life for Angie, she is not a stranger to it as her mother owned a flower shop while Angie was growing up. The biggest lesson she learned from her mom was to "always to take care of the customer." Angie has taken that lesson seriously, recounting that "this business is my legacy." The success Angie's clients find by working with her is a lifetime of learning, listening, and knowing how to treat people right.

Angie and her team deliver with excellence true executive level administrative, project management, and Human Resource support. For Angie, being able to offer small businesses and start-ups the level of support and service large corporations are accustomed to is what she finds to be the most rewarding. Alleviating small business owners of the day-to-day administrative work so they can focus on their business' main goals is the driving force behind A Squared Personal Consulting's mission and motivation.

Outside of work, Angie enjoys spending time with her fiancee, Shawn, family and friends, going to the beach as much as possible, and forever training her spoiled dog, Teddy, not to bite!

Connect with Angie Dodge:

https://www.linkedin.com/in/angie-dodge-05054a141/

8.

Deliberate Communication

Communication with a Purpose

Mark Allen | Business Coach, Training Professional for FocalPoint Business Coaching

Have you ever met someone for the first time and you just clicked right away? The conversation was easy, and you both found one another engaging – or at least it felt that way. You immediately had a connection. How did that feel? Surprisingly good, right? Maybe even great. You probably felt like you had a lot in common and that they were easy to talk to.

Now, think about a time when you met someone and conversation was, well, clunky. You just did not seem to keep their attention and you could not quite follow what they were saying or a point that they were trying to make? Think about how that felt. Not quite as good as the first encounter? You could not wait to move on? It may have even felt frustrating. I have certainly felt this before.

Now think about examples of when you had a great connection or significant **dis**connection with someone you work with. Have you given any thought as to why sometimes communication is easy, free flowing, and engaging? And conversely, sometimes, for reasons you can't quite put your finger on, a conversation with someone new is just not as satisfying? At work, it can mean the difference between great relationships and increased productivity or strained relationships that drag you down and are just plain hard and result in less productivity.

One absolute truth that we can all agree on is that communication is key to each and every kind of relationship we have in our lives – with partners, friends, kids, and of course business colleagues. This is not a new concept by any means. Consider for a minute if you invested a little bit more time and energy into being intentional and **deliberate** about communication; this includes conversations, emails, texts, etc. The key word here is deliberate. The pace of life and business is just moving too fast to slow down and plan for interactions, right?

The answer **should** be NO; things move fast, but not so fast that you can't make a critical investment. Just think about what an investment in some pre-planning could mean for you. Investing in deliberate communication garners more trust, deeper connection with people, better quality of work, increased productivity, greater satisfaction with relationships, the list goes on. Think. Plan. Be aware. Be deliberate.

Assessment Tools

To make meaningful change, you need a change of mindset AND some great insight in what to do differently. To start with, think about what a game changer it could be if you were able to operate using "The Platinum Rule." We all know the Golden Rule, right? "Treat others the way you would like to be treated." Well, "The Platinum Rule" flips the concept on its side – this rule says that we should operate under the premise that people would like to be treated how **they** want to be treated, not how **you** want to be treated.

The same goes for communication. Consider for a moment how much easier it would be for you if people communicated with **you** how **YOU** like to interact! For example, are you a little impatient when people take a long time to tell a story or get to their point? Maybe when people add a lot of colorful details and emotion to an explanation it makes you a little crazy.

For example, a simple explanation of a production issue could be so painful with too extemporaneous details. It might sound something like this:

"Let me take you back to the beginning. We got the order and we set all the details for production...you know, the order was for 1,000 units, so we had to think hard about what machine set-up to use. And you know Bob, he likes to take time to calculate runs and wants to make sure quality is good; it reflects badly on him if anything is..." and so on.

What if the people that you worked with knew you like short bullet-point communication? For example: "The machine broke one day in. It took us twice as long to complete production, so, the orders were three days late getting out."

This might seem like perfect information for you, but it may lack detail and comprehensive facts for someone else. There are many reasons why people communicate differently than others, but **<u>HOW</u>** can you know when to alter your approach and what works for one person versus another?

With more than thirty years of experience in the corporate and small business space, I have seen many tools that are aimed at revealing styles – communication styles, personality types/styles, and management styles. Each assessment tool was useful to some extent! One thing they had in common was the focus on **<u>you</u>**, the individual, and understanding your style. Many also had helpful tips on how to leverage the identified style, and how to communicate a little bit better because of this new knowledge, and some tools even drove home how knowing someone else's style might explain some of your issues communicating with them. It can be very interesting to read about yourself and understand your behavior a little more deeply, right?

Sadly, after every assessment and coaching session around the results, there came the inevitable reality – "*Nice to know, thanks a lot. I'll keep it in mind, but now I have to get back to work!*"

What I propose to you here is that thoughtful planning and deliberation about how you communicate with people can help build credibility and trust. It can also help you connect on a deeper level. This can and should result in saved time and improved relationships.

After leaving the corporate world and diving into my coaching practice, I had a renewed feeling that these tools could and should have a more meaningful use. I also learned quickly that simpler is better if you want to capture someone's attention, inspire real improvement, and achieve better results. My assessment tool of choice has become the **DISC Assessment**. **DISC** is a behavior assessment tool that focuses on four ways people react to people and to the environment around them. Specifically, how people deal with:

- Challenges and Obstacles
- Influence on others
- Pace and Change to that Pace
- Rules set by Others

Below is a simplistic and brief background on the four primary DISC styles. DISC breaks down these four distinct styles and illustrates how people may behave and communicate within their environment.

DISC is an acronym that stands for the four main personality profiles described in the DISC model: (D)ominance, (I)nfluence, (S)readiness, and (C)ompliant.

- **People with a D(ominance) style** tend to be confident and place an emphasis on accomplishing bottom-line results. They are often very self-confident, decisive, but can be blunt and impatient when communicating with others. "**D**"s are essential in a business as they are the drivers with the "just get it done" attitude and approach.
- **People with an I(nfluence)** style tend to be more open and place an emphasis on relationships and influencing or persuading others. "**I**"s are the "party" people! They are optimistic, enthusiastic, and personable. "**I**"s can be spontaneous, but maybe a bit too emotional about decisions. They can also be a bit too trusting of other people – if you say you will or want to do something an "I" takes it and runs with it.
- **People with an S(teadiness)** style tend to be dependable and place emphasis on cooperation and sincerity. When you need calm and steady, look to an "**S**"! This person is patient, collaborative, and the best listener. However, the "**S**"s are frequently those that are possessive of assignments and not quick to accept change of any kind. Slow and steady!
- **People with a C(ompliant)** style tend to place the emphasis on quality, accuracy, expertise, and

competency. "**C**"s are critical when you need solid facts and analytics. They tend to be task-oriented and can be quite the perfectionists! They are not the most trusting of people, data, or information at face value.

While we are all a blend of the four styles, inevitably, a primary style rises to the top and is how we are most often seen. Often, individuals may have a strong secondary style that tends to be more situational and comes out under stress or fatigue. The key is to understand that although a natural style may not change very much – it is who you are – with awareness and planning, you can modify your behavior to be more effective in different circumstances.

For example, my primary style is that of Influencer. I am energetic, verbose, and love any chance to talk to others (or maybe simply talk!). My wife calls me a *"big fat **I**"* – as my behavior over many years has not changed at all! I am a strong "**I**" with exceptionally low indices on all other styles. My behavior does not naturally vacillate based on my role, who I am dealing with, or the situation I am in. As a business owner, performance coach, and father, I absolutely must work at adjusting my communication for given situations. Conversely, my wife, who also spent more than thirty years in business, has always registered as a high **D**, but with a strong secondary style ("**I**") and her personality profile consistently emerged based on her roles at work and as she moved from work to home. As she became more responsible for teams of people, she adjusted and became equally as focused on the individuals and keeping teams engaged. At home, she is much more of an "**I**" and puts a great degree of her focus on people and their happiness. There is no doubt that she still makes sure things in our household get done (as a "**D**" would!) – and thank goodness she knows it cannot always be a party at our house!

How many others think like me?

The key thing to remember is that a mix of all primary styles makes the most productive and well-rounded team. In fact, the general population (or at least of those that have taken the **DISC** assessment over time) is a reasonably balanced mix:

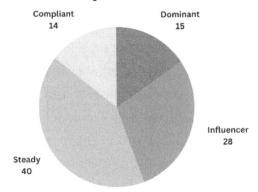

DISC Style Breakdown

Compliant
14

Dominant
15

Influencer
28

Steady
40

Thank goodness there is a mix of styles – can you imagine how much would **NOT** be accomplished if an organization were made up mostly Influencers?! It may be a lot of fun to work there, but probably would not last long if they could not accomplish tasks and were just having lively conversations all the time. Likewise, an organization with all Dominant styles may accomplish a lot and quickly, but there may be little thought as to impacts on people, long-range results, and compliance – sounds like trouble to me!

The MAGIC – Make it Useful

The point of understanding **DISC** and your own style is to understand how you approach certain situations and conversations and assess how that is different from how others may. Perception **IS** reality and if someone interprets your actions or communication as hostile, not understanding, too detailed, etc. that will absolutely dictate how they react to you. The bottom line is this: understand your style, learn the styles of others, and then modify **YOUR** communication style to fill the gaps and ease the process.

No doubt, findings from the **DISC** assessment tool are interesting, fun, and sometimes explain a bit about why people have communication challenges. As a tool, it is only as effective as the degree to which we use it everyday and make it part of a culture in our business. Although the tendency is to compare and decide which is "better," it is critical to remember that there is no right or wrong style, no style that is better or worse, and we should never encourage a mindset that certain styles are required for certain roles. In fact, the best performing teams are composed of a mix of all styles. The key is to be proud of your style, embrace others for where they are, and put the tool to work – instead of sticking the assessment in a drawer and filing it under, "That is interesting!"

The magic, I believe, is in <u>how you can use results to drive modifications in our communication based on other people's style</u>. To do this well, it requires incredibly significant and **deliberate** focus. Not just an exercise of reading a report, considering the findings, and making a one-time action plan. This is how I saw **DISC** assessments used repeatedly throughout my career. So, the concepts I present below are not tool-dependent, but can be universally applied with the right amount of motivation and deliberate focus. They are not just useful for a one time application, but rather on-going execution. Let's look at three key ways you can improve communication, relationships, and hopefully performance by deliberately planning conversations ahead of time.

1 – As a Leader

Knowing your style is critical in order to be successful as a leader. You must understand how you are seen by people, and especially, people with different or contrasting styles. Consider, for example, a leader who has a strong**D**ominant style. How do they interact with team members that are **S**teady or **C**ompliant? These interactions could make or break relationships with certain team members. As a leader, are you moving too fast? Have you provided your team with enough information, or the "why" we are moving in a particular direction? Have you solicited and considered their input? I have witnessed the demise of a career based on communication misfires – all of which I believe could have been avoided with some deeper thinking about how the other person/people perceived the communication. A few adjustments to their (the leader's) own communication would have yielded vastly different results in team performance, engagement, and culture.

Assigning roles to project work is an excellent place to use **DISC** profile information. Consider assessing team members and their style and then assigning them to roles to help improve individual and team performance. On a project where it is critical to get something accomplished in a hurry, it may be your natural tendency to assign a team of **D**ominant personality styles to make sure the project gets done. This would ensure, with high probability, that the task would be completed. But would people buy in? Would the accuracy and fiscal results be where they needed to be? Would the team be engaged and excited about those results?

I worked with an organization that needed to implement a new Human Resources Informations System (HRIS). The Senior Leadership team made the conscious decision to engage four team members with unique styles to work together and drive key aspects of the project that included the planning, testing, communicating, and implementing the new platform under very tight budgetary and time constraints. Here are how assignments were delegated:

- **Project Plan** – a team member with a **D**ominant style was assigned to set key milestones for progress and deliverables. They were allowed to set tight timelines and aggressive goals with key stakeholders, as was their nature.

- **Communication, Branding & Employee Engagement Plans** – these tasks were assigned to the strong **I**nfluencer on the team. Their role encompassed making sure the team (and all employees) were ready for the change, engaged throughout the project, understood benefits and were excited for the launch.

- **Progress Tracking** – identified a strong **S**teady style to keep the team on track. They worked behind the scenes to provide support and reallocated resources when needed. The goal being to make sure team members worked and stayed together as a unified team and made steady progress toward the aggressive goals set.

- **Testing and Quality Assurance** – the top **C**ompliant team member was assigned to develop and execute testing, auditing, and compiling results to make sure data mapping was accurate and employee records held their integrity throughout.

In the end, this project was difficult to execute and certainly had its share of bumps along the road to completion. I can attest, however, that the aggressive milestones set out by the Project team were understood from the beginning and the team rallied to find ways to achieve them. Team accountability was evident throughout, and employee engagement was high. In the end phases, the compliance team had some concerns about the number of audits being completed but ended up having extra team members jump in and volunteer for after-hours and weekend auditing. The team's efforts resulted in on-time completion of the project and it was considered successful by the organization. This example illustrates how thoughtful assignments of tasks or project work based not only on team members' roles, but also on their personality/communication styles can be highly effective.

2 – As a Team Member

Often, teams have difficulties in terms of effective communication and overall performance success. In many cases, it is a superior/boss that jumps in to assess what is going wrong and what should be done about issues. Does this always have to be the case? Absolutely not! Especially considering how much remote vs. face-to-face communication is happening now, it becomes ever more critical for team members to manage themselves to high performance rather than expecting leadership to do so and to manage through disconnects that are bound to happen on any team.

As a Team Member, you can be more personally effective, to the extent that you learn to "read the room" and identify blind spots with the team. Be observant and learn from other styles. For example, when a conflict or disconnect happens on a team, taking some time to consider the "real" reasons for the disconnect – based on the participants differing styles – could be time well spent.

Likewise, it can be very beneficial to assess first your own and then others' **DISC** type. With this information, you can then act thoughtfully to help improve cooperation and performance within the team. For example, consider how to "plug in" a team member to help work through struggles.

During tough decisions or where/when results are critical, it could be highly effective to seek out a **D**ominant team member to help get to the solution for a tough decision and for ideas on how to stay focused on results. A natural "**D**" should also consider how to jump in when someone is struggling in these areas (areas of concise decision-making and staying focused on the task at hand). This would not be the natural inclination of a **D**ominant person – they would be more focused on their own priorities and results. But with some *deliberate* assessment and/or planning, they could have a significant impact on other team members.

When creativity, vision, or inspiration is needed, team members need to look to the Influencers. An "**I**" should also pay attention and jump in to help when they see a team member lacking the creative vision necessary for a project. This does require slowing down – not a hallmark of the Influencer but a keen assessment of how they could add value where others may be struggling.

If important tasks are piling up and the resources are not lining up accordingly, a **S**teady team member can be of great support in figuring out how to pull in the right resources.

It is great when team members feel comfortable seeking an "**S**" out, but also helpful if the **S**teady team member recognizes a struggle is coming and offers to help with solutions of how to address resource needs. Steady team members can always be trusted to do quality work themselves and can be immensely helpful collaborating with team members when they have too much on their "to-do" list to be effective.

Compliant team members are organized and detail-oriented and can really keep a team on track. When organization and accuracy are required and other team members see a gap, giving forethought to how to bring the **C**ompliant member to the table and address the gap. They will help keep the group running smoothly and staying organized. When there is an issue that needs deep research or detailed work, slow down, and consider if there is a "C" on the team to assist.

3 – As a Sales Professional

Remember the Platinum Rule? The Platinum Rule most definitely applies to the selling process. How many times do you think sales have been lost due to a failure to connect with a prospective client or customer or stay connected? Probably more times than sales professionals would like to admit. If a sales professional sells *the same way* to *all* people they encounter, there are certain to be disconnects and miscommunication. If a sales professional can take time to assess a prospect's style quickly but thoughtfully, I submit that making a change to approach could mean an enormous difference in results.

Dominant

Consider this example, when encountering a prospect who appears forceful, decisive, and end-goal oriented, you are likely dealing with a **D**ominant style. The hot-button of a "**D**" is the result.

Knowing this, a sales professional <u>should</u>:

1. Be clear, specific, brief, and to the point
2. Stick to talking business – no time for personal questions and antidotes
3. Be prepared and well organized

<u>A sales professional should not:</u>

1. Talk superfluously, or about things not relevant to the situation
2. Leave any uncertainty about specifics – i.e., price, delivery timeframe, etc.
3. Appear disorganized

<u>Statements that may motivate a **D**ominant Prospect:</u>

This can give you that edge to be a leader in your industry

You can easily see the advantage this will give you

You'll want to try this. You are the kind of person that can and will make it work

Influencers

When dealing with an Influencer, you will notice their warmth, enthusiasm, and friendliness. Influencers always key in on relationships. Focus on:

1. Being warm and friendly yourself
2. Not getting into the details unless asked
3. Talk about others who can attest to your product or service

Try not to:

1. Control the conversation too much
2. Talk only about facts and statistics
3. Be short, cold or impersonal

Statements that may motivate an Influencer:

"This product will help you lead the way into the future"

"We feel this is right for you, given you are interested in new, exciting solutions"

"In fact, we'd like to showcase you as on of the businesses leaning into the future"

Steady

Like the Influencer, when you encounter a **S**teady style, they will appear warm and friendly. They may move slower and be risk-averse right out of the gate. They are about certainty and security.

<u>*As a Sales Professional, you should:*</u>

1. Start warmly, with personalized comments to break the ice
2. Present yourself and your logic, in a non-threatening way and for the team
3. Earn trust slowly – give product information and back up
4. Ask more "How" questions so they will share what they are thinking

<u>*It is best if you do not:*</u>

1. Rush the conversation, the information session, or decisions
2. Appear demanding or pressed for time
3. Force quick responses or appear at all impatient if they take time to answer questions

Statements that may motivate a Steady prospect:

"Here is some comprehensive information that will help you make a wise decision"

"This product is proven, it's been out for x years, so you know it is reliable"

"You can see our warranty eliminates risk. We stand behind our product 100%"

Compliant

Finally, when approaching a <u>C</u>ompliant style prospect, you will notice that they are conservative, analytical, in need of details and frequently refer to "data" or "stats." A <u>C</u>ompliant style is most focused on facts and does not want to be wrong about a decision.

<u>*Approach Compliant prospects by:*</u>

1. Being prepared in advance
2. Focusing on the business at hand, not personal or fluffy topics
3. Giving accurate information, providing facts, and by being realistic

You should not:

1. Be casual, informal, demonstrative, or loud
2. Waste any time with personal questions or small talk
3. Be disorganized

*Statements that may motivate a **C**ompliant prospect:*

"This is important for you. I'm happy to set up more time to go through details and alternatives"

"There has been a lot of research and thought put in on this product, which ensures it's quality"

"Once you've examined the fact, you'll see this product is right for you"

As I hope you can see, considerably different approaches can yield equally different results! When you speak to a prospect or a client in a way that helps them connect and meets them where they are, the chances of earning credibility and trust is much higher. Some thought, pre-planning, or simply being ready with modified approaches in your back pocket, can also have the extra benefit of starting a relationship on good footing. Relationships are about trust and when you make the effort to understand someone else, they are much more likely to trust you much sooner.

In conclusion

Deliberate planning on how to communicate with distinct types of people can be a powerful tool. This will help not only with relationships, but personal accomplishment, team performance, and overall job satisfaction. Relationships are critical to both our personal and organizational success.

DISC is an easy-to-apply assessment tool that provides great insight into why people behave or communicate differently. As a Leader, it provides an additional layer of intelligence that can drive more effective project management assignments. Understanding differences in styles, allows for more effective team development, team performance and helps manage through potential and real conflict among a team. As a sales professional, taking time to assess a prospect or existing client's preferred way of communicating can help in the selling and client management process considerably. The "magic" is in slowing down, assessing others, and deliberately planning for how to use **DISC** to improve **YOUR** communication.

Note to Reader:

If you are interested in integrating the **DISC Assessment tool** to help improve your or your team's communication effectiveness, boost performance or productivity, and build stronger teams, the best approach is to have a professional administer and help in the debrief process. The assessment process gives a great deal more detail than covered here and can be utilized in additional ways. If you would like further information, please contact me at mallen@focalpointcoaching.com.

Mark Allen

Mark Allen is a Business Coach and Training Professional for FocalPoint Business Coaching. His practice combines Mark's more than thirty years of business and leadership experience with the powerful results-based content and expertise of one of the world's most well-known business coaches, Brian Tracy.

Mark got his start in business helping run part of his family's manufacturing business in California. Mark then spent the majority of his corporate career honing his skills at three Fortune 100 organizations. He has a track record of leading teams through transitions, growth periods, and downturns. He has served as an executive leader overseeing numerous high volume, multi-location departments, including:

- Call Center Operations
- Customer Service and Collections
- Marketing
- Billing Statement Production and Remittance processing
- Human Resource Communications
- Benefit and Retirement Plan Administration

Mark brings a wealth of talent development, team building and leadership experience to his role as business coach. In his career, he has worked for and with all types of businesses, from large international corporations to locally owned entrepreneurships.

Throughout his life, he has learned the key factors to personal and business success: Be genuine and be unshakable in your drive and passion to achieve your goals. Mark is proud of the results he gets for his clients and is dedicated to improving business teams, creating time and generating more money.

Connect with Mark Allen:

https://www.linkedin.com/in/markallenexecutive/

http://markallen.focalpointcoaching.com

9.

Four No-Cost Ways to Leverage DEI

Fueling Retention and Performance

James Cowan | AVP, Diversity Equity and Inclusion and Next Markets Strategist

There are various differing opinions centering on the effectiveness of Diversity, Equity, and Inclusion (DEI) strategies within the context of today's evolving workplace cultures and ecosystems. In order to engage in a productive dialogue focused on practical approaches, it's helpful to start with a candid look of how DEI is often perceived within business and management circles.

Similar to Your Neighbor's Baby

As a people-management approach and business strategy, DEI may be perceived as having a lot in common with one of your neighbors' very young children. (Please humor me here and bear with this comparison; I promise it will make sense momentarily.)

Just like your neighbor's baby...

- DEI gives us good vibes, and conjures up positive thoughts about humanity and hope for the future.
- DEI may not be viewed as mature enough – yet – to truly disrupt the status quo or make a "significant" contribution to most organizations or to society, in general.
- DEI may be silently perceived as annoying to a small group of people; however, individuals who feel this way typically believe it best not to cast aspersions and go along to get along.
- DEI is initially an exciting and novel topic of conversation, eliciting positive energy and planning; however, just like your neighbor's baby, it eventually loses its luster and becomes just another "kid in the neighborhood."

Can DEI Really Make an Impact?

Although the "neighbor's baby" comparison may be a bit of a stretch, it does help to illustrate an important point. Diversity, Equity, and Inclusion is often *perceived* as a morally correct, "feel good" organizational initiative that often has minimal impact or practical application. While very few would argue that DEI-based strategies represent the "right thing to do," many fail to realize that DEI is SO much more than that! In fact, the positive, powerful impact of DEI on organizational and individual performance – as well as on business results – is proven and well-documented. For example, a recent quantitative study conducted by McKinsey and company showed that companies in the top quartile for diversity were more likely to outperform those in the bottom quartile. More specifically, ethnically diverse companies were 35% more likely to outperform less diverse companies, while gender-diverse companies were 15% more likely to outperform companies in the bottom quartile.** [12]

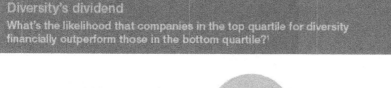

Diversity's dividend
What's the likelihood that companies in the top quartile for diversity financially outperform those in the bottom quartile?[1]

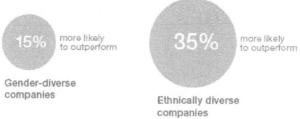

15% more likely to outperform

Gender-diverse companies

35% more likely to outperform

Ethnically diverse companies

[1]Results show likelihood of financial performance above the national industry median. Analysis is based on composite data for all countries in the data set. Results vary by individual country.
Source: McKinsey analysis

There are many data-driven and anecdotal examples that confirm the power of intentional DEI strategies and workplace diversity. These kinds of examples help to articulate the business case and the people case for Inclusion. Since Diversity, Equity and Inclusion initiatives are inherently people-driven, the business case and the people-management case are tightly intertwined. The straight-forward reality is this: **Diversity, Equity, and Inclusion drives genuine, employee engagement**. When talented people are engaged with their work and their organization – and when they feel like they have a voice – their commitment deepens and strong performance follows.

With this commitment and high performance comes a higher likelihood for collaboration. This leads to synergies across individuals and departments. Not surprisingly, it has been shown that innovation is a powerful by-product of these DEI-fueled dynamics.

Gaining Clarity: What is DEI?

A couple of months ago during an in-office work day, I was rushing to a meeting when I encountered one of our company VPs exiting the elevator. After we exchanged some quick obligatory greetings, he said, "Hey James, real quick while I have you here...can you remind me what DEI stands for again?"

That hallway exchange confirmed what I already knew: many leaders and professionals "sorta kinda" know what DEI represents and they understand the "spirit" of the concepts and terms...but they really don't have true clarity in terms of definitions and practical application. Let's clarify the acronym/term with a quick overview.

<u>Diversity: not the end game...but a critical step</u>

DIVERSITY includes all the ways in which people are different and similar; encompassing the characteristics that make an individual or group unique. While the term is often used in reference to race, ethnicity, and gender, most people and organizations embrace a broader definition that also includes - but is not limited to - the following:

- diversity of thought
- age
- national origin
- religion
- disability
- sexual orientation
- socioeconomic status
- marital status
- physical appearance

As much of the evidence-based data demonstrates, developing and nurturing a diverse organization better positions teams to meet the needs of a variety of stakeholders (including an increasingly diverse consumer population) and positions groups to win. That said, **it is important to point out that diversity in and of itself should not be the ultimate goal or the end game!** This is because it is quite possible to build and nurture a team or organization that is diverse. YET, there is still a very real possibility that the team may not be equitable, inclusive, cohesive, or innovative. Given the possibility of having a diverse team without also enjoying the inclusive utopia that we envision, it's easy to understand why diversity cannot be our ultimate goal. This "diversity without equity or inclusion" scenario also speaks to the importance of:

1. crafting a Diversity, Equity, and Inclusion strategy that is aligned with your organization's objectives and
2. being intentional about following through on identified tactics and approaches

(By the way, these approaches will likely include some versions of at least one of the four strategic tactics addressed later in this chapter.)

As we acknowledge that a diverse team does not represent the "finish line," we must also acknowledge that diversity is a critical step for teams committed to reaching the next level of high-engagement and high-performance.

Equity: one size does NOT fit all

EQUITY recognizes that individuals have different circumstances and may require different approaches to achieve an optimal or equal outcome. It ensures that fair treatment, access, opportunity, and advancement are available for all people, and not just a select few. Equity aims to eliminate barriers for various individuals and groups, primarily through specific actions, procedures, processes, and policies.

Quite frankly, the concept of "Equity" is difficult for many of us to wrap our minds around. After all, we were raised to be honest and fair people. In our minds, equity typically equates to "sameness." We should treat everyone exactly the same way, and everyone should have the exact same access to the same resources. Right?

Well...not always.

In a perfect world, it certainly makes sense that every person should receive the same resources, access, and opportunities. *Unfortunately, we don't live in a perfect world.* Giving everyone the same access often assumes that everyone has been equally equipped – professionally, generationally, educationally, and/or otherwise – to be in a position to be selected and thrive; regardless of the environment or unique circumstances.

On the other hand, equity inherently considers circumstances and environment. It's not about giving people unfair advantages to the detriment of others. Equity focuses on creating environments, teams, and organizations that places everyone in a position for success.

Implementation leans toward a customized approach that acknowledges differences and seeks solutions accordingly. Over time, approaches grounded in equity can help to enhance diversity and ensure that a wider spectrum of voices, viewpoints, and backgrounds are in the room.

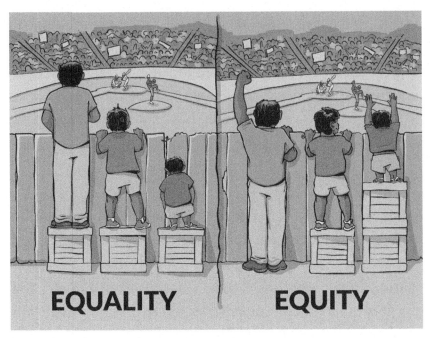

EQUALITY | **EQUITY**

Inclusion: "I'm not just in the stadium....I'm playing in the game"

INCLUSION refers to actions that create environments in which any individual or group feels welcome, respected, supported, valued, and comfortable enough to fully participate as a member of the team. An inclusive culture embraces differences, embodies respect in words and actions, and fosters diversity of thought, perspectives, and values. As organizations nurture inclusive environments, it's perfectly fair to expect that the outcome will be a culture that yields greater commitment to work, an energetic willingness to engage, and greater innovation across products and processes.

In many ways, Inclusion is the easiest concept to grasp within the DEI triad. Not only is it the simplest piece, but it is also the most universally agreed-upon piece. Very few managers or leaders question the true power of Inclusion within the context of employee engagement and retention (even if these same managers aren't exactly sure how excited they are about "Diversity" and "Equity"). That said, it's important to point out that all three terms are inextricably linked. Each one complements the other. So, as a Manager, if Inclusion is "your jam"...meaning that it is truly a management focal point that you can get behind, then it makes sense to understand and assess the role of DEI-related approaches as part of your strategic management and team-building paradigm.

Let's take a closer look at some of these DEI-based approaches that can supercharge your team's level of engagement and commitment.

Four Simple Ways to Supercharge Retention and Performance

In the Diversity, Equity, and Inclusion space, there are endless approaches and strategies that can help improve retention and engagement. In fact, diversity-practitioners confirm that many of the most successful, strategically-driven DEI frameworks are made up of approximately twenty-five or more strategic actions! (While that may seem like a large number, many of these actions may simply be more intentionally focused, time-bound versions of tactics that the company or team may have already been engaged in. This number also assumes that the broad organization has made a commitment to DEI, including at the Leadership or C-suite level.)

The approaches presented in this chapter make no assumption that you or your organization are making an all-out, strategic commitment of resources to Diversity, Equity, and Inclusion. As a matter of fact, the four concepts presented in this chapter can most certainly add value to your team members' level of engagement and commitment; regardless of whether these approaches are utilized in isolation OR as part of a larger, more strategic plan. It must be said, however, that your results are likely to be more effective and endure if these tactics are part of a comprehensive "DEI mix." (Your DEI mix is akin to a Media mix in marketing. The overall marketing effort is more effective when it is strategically spread across different media and approaches as opposed to being overly dependent on one.)

It should be clear, then, that these four approaches are not the "be all and end all" of DEI-related strategies that will positively impact retention and engagement. However, these tactics were selected within the scope of this chapter because they met at least a few of the following criteria:

1. These approaches (actions) can be implemented relatively easily with little out of pocket costs, if any. In other words, you don't need a big DEI budget.
2. They are relatively easy to outline, explain, and

remember.

3. They can be implemented in isolation or in partnership with other DEI or retention strategies
4. These approaches are particularly applicable in times of high turnover and/or low unemployment.

Now that you are sufficiently curious, let's talk about each DEI-based approach.

1) Avoid "Only-ism"

As we travel along our DEI journey, and even as we travel along life's journey, it is always wise to avoid and stamp out detrimental "isms." Clearly, the most notorious "isms" include racism and sexism. These two "isms" alone have (and, in some cases, still do) caused catastrophic harm to individuals and families, stunted the growth potential of countless careers, and even adversely impacted the mental health of many. There's another "ism" that can be insidious, primarily because of its relative lack of notoriety and attention. Additionally, this "ism" is much less common and less discussed than the others. This is the very real phenomenon of "Only-ism."

A recent article in the Harvard Business Review led with the title, "Employees are Lonelier than Ever."[3] This is especially true for women who work in male-dominant environments, people of color, and members of other marginalized groups. People in these areas are more likely to be the "only" woman in the C-suite, or the "only" black person in the office, or the "only" Asian-American attending the conference. In fact, members of some minority groups may use the term "only lonely" to refer to those potentially awkward, isolated situations/occasions where they are the "only" representative of a particular group or segment.

The concept of being the "only lonely" is not limited to race, ethnicity, or gender. It's quite possible that a valued worker could feel isolated because they are the only one who holds a particular (potentially unpopular) viewpoint. Or perhaps an individual feels isolated because they are the only one in a department who doesn't have children. It might be difficult for this person to participate in lunch conversations that some of the parents may have about Harry Potter, or about the challenges of finding quality and adequate care for their children.

While some of these examples may not appear to be earth-shattering, they contribute over time to the pervasive feelings of "Only-ism." Importantly, these dynamics can also hinder the possibility of forming quality connections at work; which can be instrumental in driving enthusiasm and commitment. Jane Dutton and her colleagues at the University of Michigan's Center for Positive Organizations characterize high quality connections as those based on empathy and interdependence.[4] How can an "only lonely" thrive in either of these areas if they feel like no one relates to or genuinely accepts that person as a valuable, contributing team member? Without high quality connections, talented individuals are more likely to look for other opportunities outside of your team.

So, how can forward-thinking leaders and managers proactively address the detrimental effects of "Only-ism" and increase the chances of retaining valuable and diverse talent? Well, awareness is the first pertinent and impactful step. As a leader, once you are more aware of the possibility that certain team members may feel "disconnected," you can then take the necessary steps to ensure that those individuals are more likely to feel included and valued. (By the way, it goes without saying that the steps you decide to take as a manager should be consistent with your personality AND your organization's culture.) That said, you and your team members should keep your collective radar up for positive, proactive (seemingly minor) activities that may help to engage a potential "only lonely."

For example:

- <u>Seek out group-specific, growth-oriented activities that your company can endorse.</u>

    One of the really great people I met, Leonard, happened to be the only African-American on the sales leadership team of his financial service company. He enjoyed his job for the most part, but was vocal about the fact that there were too few minorities in the industry at large, let alone his company. Although his organization was in the process of searching for minority talent, the process was slow. In the meantime, Allen was anxious to see evidence of his company's progress and forward trajectory. Imagine his surprise when his boss offered to send him to the Conference of African-American Financial Professionals in Tampa, Florida!

What made this scenario special wasn't the fact that Leonard attended the conference. What was most noteworthy was the fact that attending the conference was his manager's idea! As an inclusive leader, Leonard's manager recognized the importance of showing support for Leonard's career growth while facilitating his connections with other black and brown people who are walking similar paths in similar shoes. Outstanding.

- <u>Encourage and support involvement with ERGs.</u>

Employee Resource Groups (ERGs) and Affinity Groups play a critical role within the culture of many organizations. These voluntary employee groups offer opportunities for people with common identities and/ or interests to come together in the workplace for social interaction, career development, and cultural awareness events. In many organizations, ERGs are an excellent way for those who feel like "only lonelys" to connect with other like-minded individuals, form quality connections, and explore creative ways to raise DEI awareness across the larger organization.

As a manager of team members with diverse backgrounds and interests, it is your job to make it easy for team members to get involved with existing ERGs. Or, if necessary, help them to follow the appropriate internal channels to start a new one. This is a very real leadership opportunity that could help to raise the employee's commitment to your team and to the organization.

"Only-ism" on your team should be avoided whenever and wherever possible. The purpose of stamping out "only-ism" is not to discourage independent thought and action, but to establish connections that enhance our work. Amy Durham, a UC Berkeley Certified Executive Coach and the author of Create Magic at Work, sums it up this way:

> "Bringing people together – providing social support – is so important. And it's a win-win because it improves profitability and productivity, keeps retention high and helps employees stay engaged."**

2) Meetings: Make them Inclusive

Linkage Inc., a global leadership development firm committed to advancing women and accelerating inclusion in organizations, recently conducted an intriguing body of research. They set out to determine which tactics, approaches, or actions have the greatest impact on inclusion. The research methodology included in-depth interviews with HR leaders and an extensive survey of professionals across different companies. Researchers studied more than fifty-five different drivers of inclusion from executive action, to bias training, and programs to increase allies.[5] At the conclusion of their analysis, it was discovered that the driver that had the most significant positive impact on inclusion was, (drum roll please), Inclusive meetings.

Although this is probably not the most exciting research finding, it is noteworthy and encouraging because of its simplicity, cost-effectiveness, and especially its impact. The obvious question, however, is this: what exactly does an inclusive meeting look like? In conducting the research, Linkage Inc. defined an inclusive meeting as one where everyone is heard, administrative work rotates, remote employees are well included, and attendees give appropriate recognition for ideas.**

When inclusive meetings are defined with such clarity, the go-forward plan for leaders and managers becomes simple and relatively straight-forward to implement. It is important for meeting leaders to be intentional about making sure a rotating schedule is established (for different meeting facilitators, note-takers, etc.), and that less vocal attendees are pulled into the discussion in ways that are not overly pressurized. The biggest challenge for some teams will be in those environments where participative meetings are not typical. However, this is clearly a case where change and new habits are good things! By intentionally establishing a schedule and a plan and remaining committed to following them, the "new" meeting style will rapidly evolve into the "normal" meeting style.

3) Eyes on Equity

Many organizational leaders agree that they would like their workforce to mirror the population they serve. As we operate in a global economy and serve an increasingly diverse U.S. population, [see Figure 1] there are several mission-driven and business-related reasons to strive for a diverse workforce.

FIGURE 1

Annual U.S. population change, 2016 to 2021

U.S. total and select race-ethnic groups

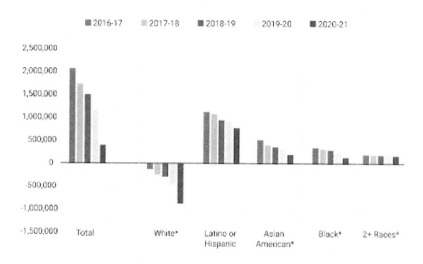

Source: William H. Frey analysis of Census Bureau population estimates July 2016 to July 2021
*Non-Hispanic members of race; Asian American includes Native Hawaiian and Other Pacific Islander

B | Brookings Metro

Despite the growth in multi-cultural consumers, achieving diversity in company leadership has been more of a challenge. For example, among Fortune 500 companies, women hold only 7% of positions at the CEO level, while ethnically diverse executives comprise 9%.[6]

The dearth of diverse leadership in companies is not a challenge that will be resolved overnight. However, a long walk always starts with the first step. As a leader or a manager, you should consider partnering with HR to identify ways to source talented women and minority candidates. Hold yourself, your colleagues, and company leadership accountable to any stated goals to be innovative or inclusive in terms of diversity-recruiting and diversity-hiring practices. Don't be afraid to seek ideas and input from your diverse team members who may be feeling like they are the "only-lonelys." These employees are likely to feel gratified that they work for a company that is taking concrete steps to add more women, minorities, and other underrepresented groups to the team.

There's a saying that is often repeated by women and minorities who aspire to greatness and higher levels within an organization: "You can't be what you can't see." Take steps toward ensuring that your team – especially your leadership team – represents a variety of different groups, segments, and backgrounds. This way, people on your team will be less likely to believe that success is impossible for them, and they will be less likely to leave your team for another organization that is representative to and for them.

- **4) Nurture Transparency among Executives and Leadership**

> *A transparent workplace promotes a two-way conversation between employees and management and openly and honestly discusses matters pertaining to business performance, goals, objectives, and more.*
>
> *Companies with transparent workplaces nurture an environment free from fear, encourage employees to be open about their achievements and mistakes, and foster a safer, more positive environment. Those who do not often feature a strenuous relationship between employees and management or executives where information is withheld, decisions are not explained, and input is not wanted.* – Mentimeter.com (September 2022)

Transparency and open communication foster trust and increase the chances that team members feel informed, empowered, and engaged. When team members have a clear understanding of the organization's direction, and even its challenges, they are more likely to be committed and invested in the team's success. It's worth noting that transparency may be critical to the retention and engagement of women, minorities, and only-lonelys, because these individuals are more likely to have developed an expectation of being excluded, at worst, or at best, developed a feeling of not being part of the mainstream.

Once again, the beauty of the transparency approach is that it is cost-effective, easy to implement, and massively impactful. It requires an intentional commitment from the Senior Leadership to keep team members in the loop...with regularity and candor.

To that end, here are a few practical suggestions that you and your leadership team might consider for implementation.

- Host regularly scheduled roundtable discussions where the CEO and/or company leadership can discuss company wins, progress, and challenges.
- Make important information available to employees; including financial statements. (If there isn't a good reason to keep it confidential, then why would you hide it?)
- Be crystal clear about the company's strategy and whether or not the company is on plan or off track. If the latter, discuss the plan for "righting the ship."
- Normalize the inclusion conversation. Make DEI an embedded part of the organization's strategy and culture by regularly discussing wins, the future vision and leadership's commitment.

If you are already taking most of these steps, congratulations! Executive transparency is probably not one of your inclusion challenges!

The four approaches discussed in this chapter are grounded in the concepts and strategies of DEI.

These low-cost actions can easily get you and your team pointed toward increasing team member commitment, retaining your talent and positioning workers for success. So remember this AMEN acronym:

- **AVOID** Only-ism
- **MEETINGS**: make them inclusive
- **EYES** on Equity
- **NURTURE** transparency (especially among Leadership)

The fact that these four approaches form an easy-to-remember acronym may help you – in some small way – to craft your game plan and share these steps with other leaders.

AMEN! All the best to you on your DEI journey to improve employee retention, engagement and productivity!

Notes

1. "54 Diversity in the Workplace Statistics to Know" Bailey Reiners. Updated Oct. 21, 2022

2. "Racially Diverse Companies Outperform Industry Norms by 35%" Ruchika Tulshyan. Forbes.com. Jan 30, 2015

3. "Employees Are Lonelier than Ever. Here's How Employers Can Help." Harvard Business Review, 27 Aug. 2021, https://hbr.org/2021/06/employees-are-lonelier-than-ever-heres-how-employers-can-help.

4. "Employees Are Lonelier than Ever. Here's How Employers Can Help." Harvard Business Review, 27 Aug. 2021, https://hbr.org/2021/06/employees-are-lonelier-than-ever-heres-how-employers-can-help.

5. "The Hard Truth about Inclusion in the Workplace: What Works (and What Doesn't)." Linkage, Inc., 11 May 2021, https://www.linkageinc.com/resource-library/the-hard-truth-about-inclusion-white-paper/.

6. Claire Zillman."The Fortune 500 Has More Female CEO's Than Ever Before," Fortune (May 16, 2019); and Crist Kolder Associates, "Volatility Report of America's Leading Companies."

James Cowan

James Cowan has over fifteen years of experience focusing on different aspects of DEI and diversity marketing. His career journey has spanned three industries: market research, healthcare and financial services. While working in market research, he consulted with Procter and Gamble on marketing to Hispanics, African-Americans and other people of color.

Between 2006 and 2014, James held marketing and management leadership roles with two hospital systems in SW Ohio. During that time, he led efforts to reach more diverse patient populations, spearheaded efforts to establish Employee Resource Groups (ERG's) and trained clinical personnel to deliver culturally competent care.

James currently serves as the Asst. Vice-President and

Diversity, Equity and Inclusion Strategy Lead for Constellation Insurance (formerly Ohio National Financial Services). In this role, he is involved in every aspect of the company's DEI journey, including corporate strategy, diversity recruiting, sales support, change management and inclusion training.

Under James' DEI leadership, Ohio National was recognized with two awards in 2022: the Diversity and Inclusion Award in Life Insurance from the American Council of Life Insurers; and the CLIMB Award from the Cincinnati Business Courier. The category of recognition for the latter was "Centering DEI as a Business Imperative."

Throughout his career, James has had a passion for servant leadership. In addition to proudly serving as Chair of the Board of Directors for The HealthCare Connection (a Federally Qualified HealthCare Center in Cincinnati), he also serves on the Board for the Council on Aging of SW Ohio.

James earned his BA in Communications and Marketing from the University of Virginia and his MBA from Northern Kentucky University. A believer in lifelong learning, Cowan is working to complete another certificate in Diversity, Equity and Inclusion through Cornell University.

In his spare time, James enjoys weight training, mentoring young men at his church and spending time with his family, including his wife, Cheryl, adult daughter Alex and his teenage son, Bryant. James is a long-time member of the Alpha Phi Alpha Fraternity, and has been a licensed Minister since 2016.

Connect with James Cowan:

https://www.linkedin.com/in/jamescowan-mba/

IO.

HR - It's a New Day!

Christie Engler | HR Executive

Over the course of my career in HR, I have encountered many situations that gave me pause. I would like to share a couple of examples to begin...

Allow me to introduce Dan (he/him). Dan worked as a customer service representative for a large risk management company for nearly four years. He was a single father and, when we met, his son was just two years old. Dan was not in a relationship with his son's mother, but the two shared custody. He was a very nice guy at work – very personable, laid back, and always willing to help others. He was knowledgeable and provided great service to all of his customers. Where Dan struggled was punctuality. He was not a morning person and was often late for his 8:00 a.m. daily start time. He also shared with me that his son did not always sleep well, so the nights were often long when his son was staying with him (something most of us parents can relate to!) Based on attendance policies spelled out in the employee handbook, Dan was put through a progressive discipline process for his tardiness. Ultimately, Dan was terminated for violations of the attendance policy.

Meet Ari (she/her). Ari spent nearly twenty years working for a small medical practice. During her tenure, Ari oversaw the reception desk, patient scheduling, billing, and assisted the physicians with administrative and personal duties. She knew the day -to-day operations in and out and, as such, she was the go-to person for nearly every question and problem. Ari was a beloved member of the staff. As time went on, she struggled with change and progress, but she always kept a positive disposition. Eventually, the spouse of one of the physicians took on an HR role for the practice. This would begin a new phase of strictness and adherence to company policy at the practice. In her seventeenth year of service to the business, Ari became very ill. She underwent a battery of tests as her doctors attempted to diagnose her condition. Various medications were prescribed and treatments were attempted. As anyone can imagine, Ari missed quite a bit of work during this time. She was exhausted, lost sleep, endured headaches...it was a very difficult period in her life. Many of her co-workers reached out and offered their support to and for her along the way. They brought meals to her home, assisted around her house, and drove her children to their activities. Given the small size of the practice, they did not offer the benefits associated with FMLA. They did, however, have a strict policy outlined in their handbook that required documentation for any medically related absence. They also had an individual in charge of HR who was very stringent to policy and less than forgiving. Despite maintaining adequate communication throughout her illness, Ari was terminated for "failure to provide a doctor's note."

The above are both true stories of real employees who I encountered throughout my career as an HR professional. They both evoke feelings of sadness and make me sick to my stomach. What's more, is that these instances happened only a few years ago.

What in the world are we, as HR professionals and companies, doing? What is going on here?!

How I Got Into HR

I got into Human Relations to help make work great for _all_ employees. That has been my mantra and my tagline for nearly twenty years. When I was only three years old, I told everyone I was going to be the President of the United States. My family was so supportive and certain I could do anything I put my mind to that my grandma specifically asked to be given the Lincoln bedroom in the White House when I moved in. At five years old, I decided I would become an attorney prior to my presidential run. This plan carried me through my high school graduation and into my first years of college. It was during an introductory HR course during my junior year at Ohio State that I found human resources. I was sitting in class one day and it just clicked – this is what I was supposed to do with my life. This was my calling. I shifted gears from future President and lawyer and pursued a master's in HR instead of a law degree. For twenty years, I have worked closely with small business owners, leaders, and employees to help shape their workplaces into compliant, productive, fun places to be. I have loved every minute of it (even when I have encountered situations like those I initially described in this chapter). Working in HR has fulfilled my passion and purpose in this life. I truly believe God has called me to do this work.

In recent years, many of my fellow HR colleagues have experienced high levels of burnout, disengagement, and defeat. Several have decided to leave the industry altogether. While HR certainly made its mark during the pandemic, it was excruciating. I am saddened by this turn of events. However, I do understand – HR is hard. People are hard. Business owners and leaders can be downright impossible. When other professionals ask me how to cope, I offer this suggestion: "*Remember why you got into HR in the first place. What is your greatest success story? Focus on the positive impact you have made to propel you into the future.*"

How Did We Get Here?

For years, HR (formerly referred to as personnel!) was deemed the law enforcement agency of the workplace. Phrases like "Oooh, HR is here – who's in trouble?" or "If HR is coming, it means someone is getting fired." and "Don't say that in front of HR!" Have you ever heard phrases such as these upon entering a room? I have – and it is beyond annoying. I'm not just "HR," I'm a person and an employee just like everyone else within a company. For some reason, HR has been dehumanized at work. The irony is...HR **is** the people!

My parents' and grandparents' advice holds true: the separation between work life and home life was to be expected. Demanded, in fact. Employees were not to bring their full authentic selves to the workplace. Come to work, forget your home and personal life at the door, do your job, collect your paycheck, and move on. Illness, obstacles and hurdles to overcome with childcare, doctor's appointments, home repairs, etc. – those were things to be dealt with outside of work hours. No one talked about employee engagement or workplace culture. The focus was on production and profits. Employees were simply the pawns that made the operations happen, yet they were viewed as expendable. A good friend of mine (and fellow HR pro) was once told by a more experienced HR leader that she needed to be "different at work than at home." Her response? "Sounds exhausting to pretend to be something that you're not." I agree wholeheartedly.

HR has also been tasked with all the administrative, tactical duties associated with employees. These tasks are quite important for reasons of compliance and employee experience. Let's face it – at the end of the day, people work for pay and benefits. We have to pay our bills and provide basic living necessities for ourselves and our families. If you could receive the same compensation and total rewards yet choose to do anything for work, would you choose your current job/career? Or would you choose to do something else? Something that really ignites your passion(s)? We cannot overlook the importance of payroll and benefits administration; most other work done within HR is fluff in comparison. However, HR is capable of doing/providing so much more for the company and its employees. We can execute the necessary administrative processes **AND** provide a strategic direction that enhances the workforce (and ultimately the results/profits) of any organization.

What Do We Do Now?

HR must lead the way for workplaces to become people-first. How do we do that? Here are my suggestions based on my experience:

1. Add the word 'empathetic' to the desired list of qualities for every member of your HR team. Seriously, put it in your job descriptions.
2. Get out of your comfort zone. "We have always done it that way" is not a strategy for progress.
3. Let people be real. We want people to bring their authentic selves to work.
4. Reconsider the purpose of HR in the world of work. We are tasked with mitigating risk while building and preserving a people-centric culture.
5. Get back to basics – HR professionals have to know their stuff. There is no point in having a laundry list

of letters after your name if you do not understand the foundational pieces of HR that keep the workforce running. Have the discipline to learn your craft. Be sure to stay informed – things in the industry change all the time!

6. Give grace. Working with people is not black and white; there are many layers of gray.

7. Remember that employees, owners, leaders, and managers – they are all people.

8. You are the advocate for the employees...so, get out there and **advocate**! HR should be a trusted confidante of the top dog in the company. Don't waste the privilege of being the emotional intelligence meter they surely need you to be.

Most importantly, HR must have support from the highest levels of leadership within the organization. Benefits, open enrollment, manager training, and performance reviews cannot be treated as just "activities of the HR department." We do not conduct these events simply and solely to check boxes. Work done by the HR department must be supported as "company-sponsored," and members of the leadership team should vocalize their support. This is the only way for employees to understand the importance of HR's role to the company in its entirety.

I worked with a small manufacturing company in Central Ohio for many years. They were a multi-generation family-owned business – very successful with low turnover and high employee engagement. Definitely one of the best work environments I had ever seen and worked with. The owner,

Jim, was humble and intelligent. A few years ago, Jim wanted to do an employee engagement survey. From the data we collected and reviewed, we found that the employees were unable to nail down the exact mission statement of the company. Jim wanted to take this opportunity to update the mission statement, as the previous one was developed when Jim's father was in charge. We decided to introduce this initiative to the employees during a regular team meeting. I insisted that Jim start the conversation and explain why this activity was important. Sure, I could have done it – but I'm not the reason these employees come to work every day. I explained to Jim that the only way to get full buy-in and participation was for him to show his support and encouragement of the task. The project was a great success – the employees helped to craft an updated mission statement that is still up on the walls to this day.

How many times has a manager come to you wanting to fire someone RIGHT NOW? TO-DAY. You ask them to walk you through the situation and request copies of the documentation that would validate the "why" that has been done to date. They produce nothing. You explain to them they cannot move forward with the termination. They get mad, storm out of your office, and go raise hell with whichever member of the leadership team will listen. You – HR – are described as "unreasonable" and "unhelpful" in this situation. Sound familiar? Now consider this: what if you take a consultative approach to how you practice HR? What if you gave **options** instead of **_directives_**? In this case, barring any legal restrictions, a manager may terminate an employee at any time for any reason (employment at will).

Now, we know that just because they **<u>can</u>** doesn't mean they **<u>should</u>**. But you want to help them reach that conclusion **<u>with</u>** you. So, you tell the manager that if he/she/they pursues the termination as it is, these are the possible outcomes. If you wait and go through the progressive discipline process...here are the other possible outcomes. You ask them: *"How much risk are you willing to take on?"* (I have asked business owners if they would prefer federal or state prison based on their actions and potential outcomes.) Instead of being stringent, you are acting as a strategic business partner. You are attempting to understand the manager's dilemma and work with him/her/them to solve it in a manner that reduces risk to the company. Now, I'm a realist and a true HR practitioner – I know not every situation will allow for this level of consultation. Some situations are very black and white. However, I see too many HR professionals that are focused solely on following policy and not supporting their people. This has to change. Again, remember, HR **<u>IS</u>** the people. HR will never achieve the recognition and respect it deserves by playing watchdog over the workplace. We have to be reasonable and find ways to add true value to an organization/company.

Let's Get Real

My dear fellow HR professionals – if you find yourself in a role with no support from top leadership or you're working in a culture that does not place top value on its employees,

I urge you to reconsider your position. After working with hundreds of small companies throughout my career, I can tell you without a doubt that you will not single-handedly be able to change the minds of those in charge. There are countless owners of small businesses in the United States who possess very "old school" ways of thinking when it comes to work and employees – management v. labor, us v. them, the need to punish and control employees, etc. Has your organization failed to embrace remote work for the fear that employees will not be as productive without the watchful eye of management? That practice is very telling of how your leadership views their employees.

You Just Never Know

In 2011, my world as I knew it was rocked. Forever changed. My younger daughter, Emily, turned one in March and was experiencing developmental delays. She had not yet hit some six-month milestones. Our pediatrician recommended an initial round of tests – hearing, vision, EEG – to begin the quest to uncover what was going on. We found she needed glasses. Within weeks of wearing them she began crawling, cruising, and eventually walking. Her EEG was somewhat abnormal, so the doctor ordered an MRI with sedation. She began an endless stream of therapies; speech, physical, occupational. It became apparent to us that Emily was displaying symptoms of autism; however, she never quite checked all the boxes. We fought for a diagnosis, seeking testing from doctors and specialists around the state of Ohio. Just after her fifth birthday in 2015, Emily was finally given a dual diagnosis of autism and intellectual disability.

We engaged a private in-home ABA therapist, who noticed Emily's tendency to have brief staring spells. Upon further investigation, it was found that she was experiencing "silent" seizures and was then diagnosed with epilepsy. We began treatment with a pediatric neurologist in Cincinnati.

Emily began attending school, and thankfully, because of her diagnosis, she was able to attend a specialized school with little added expense. After a few years, we built a house and moved our family five miles to get into one of the best school districts in the state; one that would be able to provide for both of our girls.

Emily is now twelve and just started middle school. Her cognitive ability remains that of a toddler. Despite her challenges, she is a sweet, loving, and happy child.

This experience has come with many challenges for me, my husband, and my oldest daughter. Emily requires constant care. She has a tendency to respond to any illness with fever, which of course forces her to stay home from school. For several years, we had to make multiple two-hour trips every year for her doctors' appointments. We have fought with insurance companies to have her medications and treatments covered. It has been quite the journey. As you can imagine, this situation has affected me across all aspects of my life – as a spouse, as a mother, and of course, as an employee.

Why am I sharing this? Upon initially looking at me, you would never guess I have a child with special needs. You would not know the struggle and anguish I have endured. Through it all, I have managed to build a successful career in HR. I have remained productive and accomplished, even on the hardest days. In truth, I have worn a brave face. A façade at times.

Are any of your employees putting on a brave face? Are they crumbling beneath a strong façade? The truth is that you never truly know what is going on with your people. For so long, employees were told to hide their truth, to not bring their personal lives to work. To that end, people have gotten very good at hiding things. People have lives outside of work, and guess what? Life is messy. You should assume positive intent with your employees, but also assume that they have hard things in their home and personal lives that exist outside of work. Everyone is dealing with something.

In HR, it is not our job to be nosy or imposing. It is our job to be empathetic, to be supportive, and to work to find solutions.

The Next Generation of HR

It is an interesting time for the HR industry. We definitely made a mark during the pandemic – the increased number of companies hiring for HR talent since 2020 is proof of that. We also have a number of practitioners leaving the industry, as well as the impending workforce exodus of the Baby Boomers. So, how do we grow and promote the industry to newcomers?

HR is an experience game. Degrees and certifications are great; however, no textbook is going to teach someone how to handle an employee who comes to work drunk. Or the one who brings a gun to the office. Or when a sibling calls in and impersonates an employee to steal their paychecks (all true stories!) People are not an exact science; HR professionals have to master the art of dealing with the chaos that is employees. Experience is imperative in learning how to successfully help companies to mitigate risk while creating and preserving workplace culture.

If you have the ability to offer an opportunity to a more "junior" HR professional in your organization, please do it. The reality is that our new industry members need to learn from those of us who have been around the block a time or two. They need to be able to soak up our experiences and learn and grow from the lessons we have learned. They also need experienced HR professionals to lean on – offer up your expertise! Be a mentor, get involved in your local HR networking groups, speak to HR college classes in your area, become an adjunct professor, start a blog – the possibilities are truly endless. Find something that speaks to you and run with it. What do you wish you had known when you were starting out in HR?

Final Thoughts

Given everything going on in the HR industry, ask yourself: "Why do I stay?" What can you do **today** to propel the profession forward? What do you want the future of HR to be? To look like?

For me, I am fulfilled when an employee lets me know that something I did for them or offered to them helped them and made their workday just a little bit better. Even something as simple as explaining a pay stub or walking someone through their benefit elections – these things matter. Though these items may seem small, they can have a profound impact on employees, their families, and their quality of life. As I have progressed in my career, I have found that I love helping my fellow HR professionals however I can. I really enjoy teaching and guiding the new generation. I will continue to seek out opportunities to help and support my peers throughout the remainder of my career.

Please connect with me on social media. Let us continue this conversation and work together to make HR the best profession there is.

Christie Engler

"I got into HR to make work great for all employees. Work is the one thing most of us have in common. Life is too short not to pursue your passion and purpose." – Christie Engler

Christie Engler has been a Human Resources practitioner for twenty years with a focus on small and family-owned businesses.

Christie is dedicated to advancing the HR profession and assisting fellow practitioners. She has spoken at numerous state and local HR conferences, including the SHRM Annual Conference and Exposition in 2021 in Las Vegas. Her topics focus on providing resources and support to those working in small businesses, departments of one, and those new to HR. Christie writes a blog entitled "Living in the Gray" designed to inspire HR professionals.

Christie has worked hand-in-hand with business owners across a variety of industries. She understands the unique needs of entrepreneurs and how to best partner with them to achieve "people-first" outcomes and grow businesses. She believes managers are the front line of company culture and regularly provides training to support those leading employees.

Christie is a graduate of the Ohio State University and the Keller Graduate School of Management. She holds a Bachelor of Arts degree in Political Science and a Masters of Human Resource Management, as well as the SPHR and SHRM-CP certifications. Christie is a member of the Human Resources Association of Central Ohio (HRACO) and SHRM. Christie is an active member of the HR Unite! Community and has been featured on the HR SocialHour podcast.

Christie lives in the Columbus, Ohio area with her husband and two daughters. She is a fanatic of Ohio State football and OrangeTheory Fitness. She is a member of Prince of Peace Lutheran Church in Dublin, Ohio, and she sits on the board of directors of Habitat for Humanity of Delaware and Union Counties. Christie is an initiated member of the Alpha Xi chapter of Alpha Delta Pi sorority.

Connect with Christie Engler:

https://www.linkedin.com/in/christie-engler/

Email – christieengler@gmail.com

Twitter – @christie_engler

II.

Why Am I Not Attractive?

Connor Hopkins | Employee Benefits Consultant at McGohan Brabender

"Business is all about people. Products are developed and innovated by people, manufactured by people, produced by people, packaged by people, bought by people, sold by people, and thrown away by people. Business has always been about people, and by the grace of God, always will be." – Scott McGohan, CEO
McGohan Brabender

People are at the forefront of everything we do as employers. Regardless of your service or product, if it weren't for those creating the service or product, selling the service or product, delivering on the service or product, and administering the service or product, there would be no business at all. People are the largest investment for any company to make both literally and figuratively. For most companies, the largest line item each year is the payroll: paying your people. After payroll, the next two largest employer expenditures tend to differ by industry, but consistently fall to healthcare benefits and equipment. Yet, healthcare benefits tend to be perceived as a burden as opposed to an asset.

The hard part about benefits is that people under-appreciate them, or possibly don't even give them any attention at all, unless something negative has happened with themselves or a family member that is covered; or not covered. So, instead of educating ourselves about how to utilize our benefits and what they can do for us, they are put on the back burner until they are needed. That is just human nature. This is becoming more and more apparent as new generations enter the workforce. As younger people start their career, they tend to look at one thing: "How much money are you going to pay me per year?"

I am unapologetically a Millennial and I have seen this line of thinking, or mentality, firsthand. A classmate and friend of mine was looking for a job right out of college and accepted a job that, at the time, seemed like a lucrative position. He was making almost double what I was, with flexible work hours, PTO, etc. He was on top of the world and, to be honest, it had me wondering if I was in the right position. Should I be making more money? Will I have the same luxuries as my friend if I go somewhere else? Does the company I work for now not value us as employees? Why am I not at Happy Hour at 3:30 p.m. on a Friday like the rest of my friends? These are dangerous thoughts to have and can lead people to make rash decisions.

What my friend failed to realize was that while working as

a 1099 employee, he was not offered the same employer-sponsored benefits as those who were a W2 employee. The money he was offered was great, and with the extra money he can afford medical expenses, right? His plan worked in his favor for about four years. With all the extra money he was making, he picked up golf as a hobby. A few rounds of golf per week and an MRI later, and he found out that he had a slipped disk in his neck.

Now luckily my friend was smart enough to purchase an individual health plan, but what kind of insurance does a healthy, 25-year-old purchase on their own? You guessed it! The least expensive plan. I'll let you do the math on a $5k deductible with 50/50 coinsurance with an out-of-pocket maximum of $15k for a $30k claim. Presumably, your options are as follows: pay your life savings on treatment, or live in pain for the foreseeable future?

Obviously, this story is an extreme example, and luckily, my friend is doing just fine. However, it can be a harsh reality for a lot of people. Not only did my friend fail to realize why having healthcare benefits cost so much, but he had zero support or guidance from anyone on how to utilize his benefits to his advantage. Now, how do you think my friend felt about his position after navigating through all of this? Do you think that he felt it was sustainable to keep working in the same role? It should come as no surprise that he left for a role with better benefits.

There are many studies around the Great Resignation and the war for talent is real. With COVID, the timeline for the Boomer Generation to retire has come earlier than expected. For the first time in our lifetime, we have five generations working at the same time and what is important to each generation differs greatly.

Recruiting and retaining the right people is imperative to the growth and culture of an organization. People are already an employers' largest investment between payroll and healthcare benefits. As employers, what are you doing to educate your employees to become better healthcare consumers? Is there an opportunity to view benefits as an asset as opposed to a burden? How can I, as an employer, utilize what I already pay for to enrich the culture within my organization?

At my company, we refer to this as "The Member Journey."

Communication

Question for employers: Which employer are you?

1. **Employer 1**: "It's time for open enrollment again this year!! Our benefits aren't changing this year so we will not be holding a formal open enrollment. Just fill out your enrollment form with your elections and turn it in to HR."
2. **Employer 2**: "It's time for open enrollment again this year!! Although our benefits are not changing much, we are bringing in our partners to sit down and update

us on any changes and help to better understand the plan. They are available to meet with you one on one to discuss which option is the best option for you and your family."

If you are Employer 1, don't worry. You are not alone.

The company I work for surveyed employees from the clients we represent and asked what was important to them when evaluating their benefits package. This includes all industries, company sizes, and different generations. We, as McGohan Barbender called it "2022 Member Journey Qualitative & Quantitative Research Analysis." One of the Key Research Findings regarding drivers of member issues/anxiety are:

- Making enrollment decisions about which plans are "right for me"
- First time enrollment in high deductible health plans
- Understanding and expectations around preventative/diagnostic procedures
- Making the smart Rx drug purchases

In the study, employees were asked:

> "How much do you agree or disagree with the following statement: 'I understand most insurance terminology including deductible, co-pay, co-insurance, etc. on a scale of Agree Completely to Disagree Completely.'"

The highest results were those over the age of 65 and only 50.65% of respondents said they "Completely Agree." For those between the ages of 18-24, only 21.5% of those said that they "Completely Agreed." Prior to this study, I used to think that the younger population would be okay and just ask the older population for assistance. But knowing that only about half of the older population "Completely Agree," I am more worried that only roughly 1 of 5 younger employees truly understands for themselves.

One big mistake we often see is that employers forgo open enrollment each year. They posit: "If our coverage isn't changing, why would we need to have open enrollment? Our employees never pay attention during open enrollment anyway." For most companies, open enrollment is the only time of the year where they discuss the healthcare benefits with their employees and yet it is still glossed over. You are making a huge investment of your company by offering your employees coverage. Why not take full advantage of the investment you are making?

Your annual open enrollment is a perfect opportunity for you to educate your employees on the investment the company is making on their behalf. Total Compensation Reports are a trending strategy for employers to utilize in their recruitment and retainment strategies and tend to be distributed during open enrollment. Most employees do not realize that employers pay for at least 50% of the healthcare premiums every year. Companies will pay 100% of the premiums for other coverages such as disability or life insurance, but do employees understand that is abnormal and realize how much that would typically cost for a company? Probably not.

Take that one step further.

- Do you think your employees know who to go to when they have issues with their benefits?
- Do you think your employees understand that there is an Employee Assistance Program, or EAP, in place for them to utilize?
- Do your employees know that preventative coverage is covered in full and what all qualifies as preventative coverage?

Now, if you are Employer 2, how much of the open enrollment meeting do you feel your employees comprehend and how much do they remember ten minutes after open enrollment is over?

This is why we believe that having a communication strategy in place is so imperative. For instance, when an employee goes on vacation, do you think they know how to see a doctor in their network or how to fill a prescription since they are out of town and away from home? What if, before Spring Break – or any other holiday/break – season, employees received a flyer or video outlining how/what to do in these scenarios while on vacation? If I were a parent with a child on a prescription, I would be paying attention to that message.

To make things even more complicated, let's go back to the generational shift. We have five different generations in the workforce today. All at the same time. The older generations are just finally getting used to receiving information via email. For the younger generations joining the workforce, they may not even open an email notification and would prefer a text message. There are hundreds of technology-based solutions available to facilitate communication to your employees the way **they** would prefer to receive it, most of which are little-to-no cost to employers.

You may be wondering, "*Is this guy's answer really just to have open enrollment meetings?*" Well, kind of. It is more of a mindset around building out an effective communication strategy to distribute throughout the year, so employees do not feel alone in the times when they need help the most.

The point here is to ask yourself: "*What are you doing to create awareness around the benefits already offered?*" This is all a part of "The Member Journey."

Engagement

Now that our employees are more aware of the benefits offered and how to understand them better or get clarification with a communication strategy, it is time to get them to buy **into** the benefits and become better healthcare consumers.

As stated previously, a large issue with benefits packages seem to be that nobody utilizes the benefits unless something negative has happened, hence the negative connotation. Employee engagement is the key factor in one of the main complaints of benefits: the cost. In the same study mentioned earlier, we found that "The Member Journey" only has a few delights, and the delights stem from "getting something for free," or, for cheaper. We all know how expensive it can be, but there are some different strategies to utilize to help maintain the cost.

A trending strategy we see is an Incentivized Wellness Initiative such as gift cards for preventative screenings, reduced premiums for wellness compliance, or even a surcharge for those out of wellness compliance. While a step challenge among employees is a fun activity to do, initiatives around preventative care tend to have a larger impact on what employees care most about: the cost. At the company I work for, if employees do not have an annual physical and an annual Biometric Screening, we pay a higher percentage of the overall premiums than those that do.

In the article "How Preventative Care Lowers Health Care Costs" by Kimberly Amadeo it is noted that "Four out of the five leading causes of death are caused by chronic diseases that are either preventable or likely to be manageable with regular access to health care: Heart Disease, Cancer, Chronic Lower Respiratory Disease, Stroke." [1]. The vast majority of companies do not have a policy for preventative care. Does yours?

Encouraging employees to find a Primary Care Physician is a good step in the right direction and very cost effective for employees. In fact, it's free. Do you know how many of your employees are seeing their Primary Care Physician on an annual basis? According to a report published in JAMA Internal Medicine, fewer Americans had a primary care provider in 2015 than in 2002. The overall proportion dropped from 77% to 75%.[2]

Biometric Screenings take it another step further. Biometric Screenings give employees instant results on those causes of deaths mentioned above and tests for things such as cholesterol, blood sugar, blood pressures, body fat, body mass index, etc. Some employers offer Biometric Screenings onsite to promote and drive employee participation.

I have a good family friend whose life was saved after doing a preventative Biometric Screening. He is a healthy guy, he isn't overweight, and he works out regularly. After a screening it was noticed that some of his numbers were off the charts, and it didn't make any sense. He was taken to the hospital and found a 97% blockage in one of the arteries leading to his heart. If he would have waited longer or never received a screening, who knows what could have happened?

Imagine getting to a point where your company's annual high claimants, such as a heart attack, were contained and treated as just high blood pressure. Not only does it impact the cost of your plans, but the internal morale within the company.

Culture

"Company Culture is the collective attitudes, beliefs, and behaviors of a company and its employees and how they relate to the actions of the business. It impacts company operations, strategic planning, and ultimately the overall performance of the organization." So, what are your company's collective attitudes, beliefs, and behaviors on your benefit package? [3]

People are a company's biggest asset. A company's culture is a direct reflection of the people. Companies continue to preach how strong of a culture they have, but what are they actually doing to fulfill the culture that they are portraying?

When we talk about company culture, we consistently speak of the topics that can positively increase a company culture. PTO, flexible work schedules, remote work, and monthly pizza parties certainly help with company culture. However we tend to only focus on the positives of company culture and do not look at what a negative company culture can do.

Forbes released an article titled, "The Five Most Common Culture Problems – And Their Solutions," stating that the five most common culture problems are as follows:

1. Employees are bored, discouraged, and/or generally unhappy.
2. Supervisors are under-equipped, so they over-supervise.
3. **Turnover is too high.**

4. Conflict or tension is palpable.
5. Communication only flows down, and not up[4]

"In another article titled "Top 15 Reasons Your Employees Stay" the top three reasons are: Growth and Development, Good Pay and Benefits, and Integrity.[5]

The goal of this chapter is to provoke employers to think differently in their approach around employee benefits, learn how to utilize those benefits to attract the best talent for the company, and keep the best talent within the company.

Ask yourself as an employer: "Am I *utilizing our second largest spend to my advantage? Or am I going through the motions and simply hoping that employees understand the value on their own?*"

So, "Why Am I Not Attractive?" Is it because employees don't care? Or is it because we – as a company – are failing to educate, communicate, and engage employees on what they can do for them? Look inward, and do some internal digging. Then, you tell me.

_____

Notes

1. Amadeo, Kimberly. "How Preventive Care Lowers Health Care Costs." The Balance, https://www.thebalancemoney.com/preventive-care-how-it-lowers-aca-costs-3306074#:~:text=When%20patients%20have%20regular%20access,have%20progressed%20past%20regular%20management.

2. "Fewer Americans Have Primary Care Providers." Fewer Americans Have Primary Care Providers | ASH Clinical News | American Society of Hematology, American Society of Hematology, 2022, https://ashpublications.org/ashclinicalnews/news/4901/Fewer-Americans-Have-Primary-Care-Providers.

3. Beasley, Charlette, and Jennifer Hartman. "What Is Company Culture? Definition, Examples & Tips." Fit Small Business, Fit Small Business, 3 Jan. 2023, https://fitsmallbusiness.com/what-is-company-culture/.

4. Ryan, Liz. "The Five Most Common Culture Problems -- and Their Solutions." Forbes, Forbes Magazine, 15 Aug. 2016, https://www.forbes.com/sites/lizryan/2016/08/13/the-five-most-common-culture-problems-and-their-solutions/?sh=314d0ff29bed.

5. Sunshine, Beth. "Top 15 Reasons Your Employees Stay [Infographic]." Top 15 Reasons Your Employees Stay [INFOGRAPHIC], https://blog.thecenterforsalesstrategy.com/infographic-top-15-reasons-your-employees-stay.

Connor Hopkins

Connor Hopkins often considers himself the luckiest man in the world, being married to his wife, Erica, who works as a Special Education Teacher. Outside of work, Connor is an avid Cincinnati Sports Fan, a bourbon enthusiast, and an animal lover. Connor and Erica live with their dog, Joey Burrow, and their two cats, Cincy and Ja'Marr. (Who Dey!)

Connor was born in Dayton, OH, and currently resides in Cincinnati, OH, after graduating from the Lindner College of Business at the University of Cincinnati. While in high school and college, Connor coached middle and high school lacrosse and is passionate about educating our future leaders.

Upon graduation, Connor started in the Staffing and Recruiting Industry, where he worked directly with HR

Professionals and Leadership Teams to help build a sustainable workforce with a strong culture.

He now works as an Employee Benefits Broker, where he partners with Finance and HR teams to develop the most optimal and cost-effective employee benefits package for employers to offer their employees. With over eight years of experience partnering with HR Departments and Executive Leadership Teams, he has seen first-hand what it takes to establish and maintain a strong company culture.

Connor's mentor and hero in life is his father, Van Hopkins, who was a small business owner in Dayton, OH. Van started as a Lot Tech at a dealership and, after more than thirty years of hard work, became the owner of his own dealership: The American dream. This drove Connor's passion for finding a career where he can help small and medium-size businesses.

Connect with Connor Hopkins:

https://www.linkedin.com/in/connorhopkins/

12.

It's Not Enough to Say, "People Count"

It Takes Work

Bonita Palmer | Certified Business Coach, Owner ActionCOACH

Every good employer, no matter the size of the business, wants to believe their people are their greatest commodity. It's not enough to believe it. There must be evidence of it. Unfortunately, most employers don't realize that a nice salary and benefits package doesn't make people feel like they count. It's not enough to write it into a company's core values and culture statements if no action is taken. To truly make people feel like they count is to weave them into the fabric of the organization. The taller the organizational chart, the harder it becomes to accomplish this. It becomes more difficult to get buy-in and make the front-line team feel like **_more_** than just cogs in the machine.

If an organization wants to benefit from everyone being invested and delivering consistent results, it takes some real effort. It might mean taking a good honest look in the mirror, shifting the mindset, and thinking about the business differently. It also means opening up to identifying opportunity areas in the business to make it more employee focused. When you have the right people in place and you support them, they will deliver the desired results.

I spent several years working in Corporate America before stepping away and starting my own business. I worked in Operations for large contact centers in Insurance and Banking. I started on the front-line as an inbound customer service representative in Disability Insurance. Less than a year later, I was certified as a Business Trainer for new customer service representatives. I served as an Interim Supervisor for the classes I trained and eventually was placed as a permanent Supervisor. Initially, I had a team in Disability and later transitioned to Property and Casualty. My final promotion before leaving the insurance industry was to a Business Manager role. When it was time to move on, I took the role of Regional Service Manager in a large banking contact center. I had many years to observe what these organizations did to demonstrate how their people counted. Now, as a small business owner and a coach, I've taken time to reflect on what worked well or what didn't; or what failed completely.

Contact centers are very high-stress atmospheres and there are typically a lot of seats to fill. It tends to be a fairly negative work environment with high turnover. Key Performance Indicators, or KPIs, and results are used to determine annual increases and bonuses. The results are tied to the company goals starting with your front-line team. If they deliver poor results, it has a ripple effect up the corporate ladder. It leads to pressure placed on the Senior Leadership team, who then pressures the Mid-Leadership team, who then pressures the front-line team and suddenly no one counts anymore. Here's the great news: it doesn't have to be that way. The less than great news is the lack of acknowledgement of the root of the problem. So, what is the root of the problem? It lies within fractured systems that don't support attracting the **right** people, the intentional selection process, proper training, or continuity of employee engagement. The front-line team is "patient zero," and it's where we should start making people count.

Let's examine the journey of a front-line employee and expose the eight opportunities for a breakdown in the process of making sure people truly count.

The Decision to Hire

Having a "people-count" attitude starts even before the recruitment process. After all, we want to hire the right people from the very beginning. First, some questions need to be answered. What attracts the right people? How do we recruit the right people? We start by looking at the entire recruitment process. We want to recruit talent, not fill a slot with a want ad. Recruiting is all about marketing. We market our business for a target customer, so we should also be marketing our business for the ideal employee. It's no longer just about money for a potential-hire, anymore. When you think about spending eight hours of the day working for someone else, it's about the "WIIFM" (what's in it for me?). Prospective employees want to know **why** they should work for **us** rather than work for our competitor. What can we offer employees that our competitor can't? What is unique about working for us?

Think of it like this:

> I own a landscaping company. Like my competitors, I hire contractors (1099s). Just like my competitors, I offer a competitive wage, guaranteed forty-hour work weeks, dependable hours, a paid vacation, and no weekend-work. How can I set myself apart from my competitors and attract good employees? Most people who apply are young, healthy, and need some type of medical insurance, but they can't afford the marketplace. My competitors don't offer insurance and neither do I. However, I found an affordable insurance option I can share with my employees should they choose to get coverage.

I've just set myself apart from my competitors with a marketing strategy and it didn't cost me anything extra!

Not only do prospective new-hires want to know what sets us apart from other employers, but they want to know about the company culture; how flexible is the schedule, is it a remote position, is there upward mobility, are there learning opportunities for personal/professional growth and advancement? It's no longer just about money or title; it's about the work environment.

Positional Contracts

As a coach, I encourage business owners and leaders to develop positional contracts. The concept came from the EMyth system. This system is designed to help each person understand how their work affects the company as a whole. Think of it as a job description on steroids. With positional contracts each person knows what they are expected to do, how they are expected to do it, and when it's expected to be completed. Positional contracts include characteristics, skills, and qualities needed for the job. It's robust with information you don't ordinarily see in a basic job description. Positional contracts can help develop a strong recruitment advertisement that attracts the right talent. Candidates that aren't a match will deselect themselves before even entering the hiring process.

The Recruiter

The recruiter should be the first point of exclusion. As an onboarding leader at both the insurance company and the bank, I had many conversations with the recruiters during the hiring seasons. The vigor of the weeding out process on the first phone interview was directly related to the number of seats we had to fill. Fewer seats meant a more hearty conversation. If there were a lot of seats to fill, it was less about the conversation and more about simply filling the position with someone. Anyone. When the goal is quantity over quality, less attention is given to detail. When there is less attention to detail, there is a greater risk of bringing candidates into the interview process that otherwise may not have made the cut. If we need to fill twenty positions but we only have ten really good candidates, go for quality. Hiring is expensive. We don't want to pull in people who aren't a good fit because we will eventually have to replace them. More importantly, the ten good quality candidates could become collateral damage. Their experience is impacted by the less capable employees. Hiring those who actually fit must be the first point of exclusion.

The Interviewer

The interview process can often be the source of the biggest breakdown. The reason being that, most likely, we don't properly train those who interview potential employees. When we send a supervisor into an interview with a packet of questions, it's not enough.

When I was at the bank, the front-line supervisors did the face-to-face interviewing and made the hiring decisions. It was a noble concept. These people were going to report directly to them. It made the most sense and it seemed fair that they should get to pick who they wanted on their team. The problem with this model lies in the reality that there was no training on how to conduct an interview and choose quality candidates.

I sat in on a few such interviews.

One I remember vividly:

A nice, well dressed, well spoken young man was interviewing for an inbound customer service position. I sat quietly and listened as the supervisor checked all the boxes by asking all the questions in the interview packet. I noticed she indicated on the packet she was going to give a favorable response to the recruiter to hire him. I asked politely if she minded if I asked him a few questions. She agreed.

First, I asked if he had ever been exposed to a contact center before that day and he responded "No."

I asked if he understood what this job really looked like on a day-to-day basis. His reply was, "Answering customer calls." He clearly had no idea what to expect out of the job or his daily responsibilities/tasks should he choose to join the team. So, I took it upon myself to enlighten him.

I explained, "When you come in each day, you plug your headset into the phone and you are tethered to it for two hours. Then you get a fifteen-minute break to go to the restroom and get a snack or a drink. You return and are tethered to your phone for a couple more hours and then you get thirty minutes for lunch. You come back and are tethered to your phone for another couple of hours and then get another fifteen minute break. You come back and are tethered to your phone again until the end of your shift. I wanted him to feel the restriction of the position. When I asked his thoughts, he told me he was a musician and many times spent eight to ten hours a day at his keyboard without getting up. I followed up asking him if music was his passion, to which he replied, "Yes." I then asked if he had the same passion for answering phone calls from people who are not calling to say "Thank you for taking such good care of my money." I explained that, more often than not, they are calling to complain about something." His response was weak. The supervisor conducting the interview still decided to have the recruiter make him an offer. I drew a six on the corner of his interview packet. When the supervisor asked why I did this, I told her that that's how many months it will be before he quits. Almost six months to the day, he just stopped coming in to work. He didn't even bother to give notice or tell her he was quitting. She hired him because she thought he was a nice guy with some good customer service experience, and he was. He was **NOT** a good candidate for the role he was hired for, and she missed that point entirely.

The interview process is far too important. It's a skill that should be taught and one that should be practiced. Often. Interviewing is about learning how to identify red flags, knowing what questions you can, and **_can't_**, ask and being prepared to respond appropriately when the interview goes off-script. Because it will! Most importantly, it means deciding to hire based on fitness for the position, not just because they interviewed well. When it comes to the interview process, not everyone is cut out to do it and that's okay. Choose those people wisely.

Onboarding and Company Introduction

The company onboarding process is where the magic begins. Company culture should play a big role in building relationships with new-hires. Culture and the relationships lay the foundation for employee involvement and engagement. Now is the time to make an authentic impression on new team members. Give them a sense of how important they truly are to the organization rather than making them feel like just another cog in the wheel. Being authentic is the key. Team building activities should give a sense of camaraderie but also an understanding of accountability and order. We are here to do a job and do it well, but we are in this together as a team. Now is **not** the time to put on a false façade. They have interviewed and said "yes" to the offer. So, be honest and keep it real.

Training

This is an area where a major breakdown can occur. As trainers in the Insurance Industry we trained only the product we knew. I was hired into the Disability department and trained as an inbound customer service representative. I answered questions and helped people with their short-term and long-term disability as well as FMLA. When I was certified as a Business Trainer, I was trained to deliver curriculum in general. When I started training new-hires, I only trained Disability new-hires. I'd been on the phones answering that call type for a year. I was able to deliver the content in training in a confident manner. I was able to answer tough questions that came up in the classroom because I had experienced the things that trainees were asking about. I knew the material and I had the practical experience to back up the material; and that combination gave me the power. You would never see me training a property and casualty class of new hires. I could have delivered the curriculum, but because I didn't have the experience of taking that call-type, I couldn't confidently answer questions or offer more in-depth explanations to assist with knowledge transfer.

Now, let's fast forward to my time at the bank. There was a training department with trainers who didn't have experience on the phones. They simply delivered the curriculum. When a tough question arose, the response would be, "Ask your supervisor when you are out on the floor." There was no practical knowledge for the trainers to pull from if a concept didn't translate from the material to the trainer down to the trainees. The trainers were not well versed in the actual practice of the job, they appeared less confident and, as a result, typically didn't have leadership power in the classroom. We hired a new class every month and with every class there was unnecessary drama because the trainers had no control over the classroom setting.

If the trainer is simply a delivery conduit for content and not a subject-matter-expert, challenges will arise. They aren't properly equipped to successfully lead a class and produce confident team members. Training, like interviewing, is a skill. Not only should a trainer be able to identify when there is a block in the learning process, they should be flexible and be able to pivot and provide understanding through their own practical knowledge of the subject matter. Working from a training module without the benefit of mastering the subject matter is a recipe for disaster and results in sending poorly equipped new hires to help customers.

Another gap in the training process is accountability. It's been my experience that trainers aren't held accountable for how the new hires execute when released from training and sent to do their job. When there is no accountability for the learning, is there any ownership for success? This can be where the ripple effect of poor results starts. If the trainer is only accountable for delivering the curriculum, why would they care about the outcome of the learning. If they are held accountable by some metric of the new hire would there be more ownership for the success of the new hire? Isn't that an interesting concept?

Ongoing Support

If there is a breakdown in any of the processes mentioned above, the ongoing support is even more critical. Ongoing support is provided in a myriad of ways and comes from all levels within the organization, not just a direct supervisor. Coaching is a **MUST** for ongoing support. One-to-one coaching and team coaching are some of the best ways to advocate for your team. Exploring not only how they perform individually, but how they interact with each other. If coaching isn't happening, disengagement surely will. Providing continuous feedback, both positive and constructive, must happen. Demonstrate understanding and correct behaviors in a teachable way. This means holding your teams accountable for their actions and their results. Remember, if they have been set up to fail by any of the broken processes mentioned above, factor that into how the coaching moment unfolds. Ongoing support also includes recognition and celebration of your team members. Even the smallest achievements should be celebrated!

Coaching is just one part of ongoing support. Providing the opportunity for continuing education, personal development, and growth is just as important. If we aren't learning, we aren't growing. Keeping our teams learning keeps them engaged and invested.

I recently listened to Eduardo Brecino's TedTalk discussing "The Learning Zone" and "The Performance Zone." He discusses the concept of the two-year plateau of employees. If we don't spend time in "The Learning Zone" continuing education and personal development, and only spend time in "The Performance Zone", then after about two years, there is a plateau. Meaning, the two-year mark is where you find employees becoming less engaged and starting to become stagnant. They stop learning and become simply adequate at what they do without growth. Maybe that's why we see so many people changing jobs every couple of years. Are they suffocating in stagnation because they lack the opportunity to thrive?[1]

Anything we can do to make our teams feel they are an integral part of our business will help them to feel, and subsequently, be more invested. They will feel like they matter and what do they counts. When your team feels supported, they'll reciprocate those feelings with your customers. When people are excited, engaged, and feel like what they do matters, the customer(s) will feel it too.

Leaders

My final process critical to helping people feel like they count is leadership. Good leaders know how to build ownership and accountability within a team. They also know how to listen, understand, and provide balanced feedback. They do all this while making team members feel acknowledged. Finding this type of leader can be a challenge. Promoting from within to find good leaders for your team/business is **not** always the answer. It can be a great motivator if it's done with intention.

I was a leader promoted from within, but I was tested. As I mentioned before, I started in an entry level role in the contact center. When I met with my boss for the first time to receive coaching, I was honest with him. I had absolutely zero interest in answering the phones. I asked him straight up what I needed to do to get moved off the phones. His response was, be at the top of the team every month. I made it my mission to do just that. However, I did more than that; I went beyond just being **really** good at my job. I asked for a mentor from another department who was in a leadership role. I joined Toastmasters. I asked to attend trainings and opportunities to learn about leadership. I did more than just my job on the phones; I developed and I grew both professionally and personally. I earned the opportunity to get Business Trainer Certification and become a trainer. I worked hard and earned the opportunity to serve as an interim supervisor and worked on special projects so I could continue to learn and grow. Because of all of this, I was promoted to Supervisor and then to Business Manager; and not just because I was great on the phones and a subject-matter-expert, it was because I worked hard on myself and not just on the job.

Putting someone into a leadership role because they are a good performer sets them and their future team up for failure. Being good at your job does not make you a good leader. I've seen many supervisory and management roles filled in just this way and, as such, have witnessed some very unpleasant outcomes. Leadership is a muscle that needs to be built and exercised. For some it comes more naturally than others. Slapping the leadership title on a person does not **make** them a good leader. If you put the wrong person in a lead role for a team, it can end up leading to a devastating outcome. High performing teams with motivated and energetic people can drop in their performance and increase their negativity. Simply because someone who had not been properly prepared to lead was put in a leadership role on the team.

Successful execution of the eight processes is a solid start. Modeling the behaviors that make people **truly** count should be the mission. As business owners and leaders, we must be good stewards of our people. Being a good steward is not just an item on the to do list. It's about culture. Employees with a purpose are more engaged and typically perform better. There is less time spent gossiping, avoiding work, and less negativity. But how do we build that culture?

A good place to start is with these simple steps.

1. Have good leaders in place. Be intentional when filling the role.
2. Have a common goal. It bonds a team.
3. Everyone needs to know the rules of the game.
4. Have an action plan. Everyone should know the intended outcome and how the team is going to get to that intended outcome.
5. Be sure to support risk taking.
6. The people who do the job every day know what works

and what doesn't better than anyone else. Challenge them to come up with new ideas and processes, then test them and measure the outcome.

7. Advocate for 100% involvement and inclusion. If someone is separating from the team or not participating, identify and address it quickly and intervene in a supportive manner.

8. Intentional ongoing training for the leader and the team is a must. In business, and in life, if we aren't learning we aren't growing. Think back to my previous example regarding the two-year plateau. The first year is spent really learning the job, the second year is spent honing the learned-skills to be the best you can be. If there is no development, growth stops. Why do you suppose some industries have mandatory Continuing Education Units (CEUs)? Because they want people to continue to grow and learn to stay engaged.

9. Good communication is a must if we are going to keep our team members engaged and feeling like they matter. Verbal communication is preferred over email. There is too much room for emotional misinterpretation in an email. We want communication that involves listening to understand, not just listening to respond. A strong argument for why the word **SILENT** has the same letters as the word **LISTEN**.

In closing, when I look back on my corporate experience there, it was difficult. I thought, because they always talked about how much people counted, it meant that I counted, too. However, the reality is that the environment changed me and not in a good way. One Christmas when my daughter was home from college, I was so excited to have the whole family under the same roof again. One evening, my husband pulled me aside and he told me, in a very loving way, that something had to change. He said I'd become so negative and internally angry that no one wanted to be around me...not even my kids. That conversation cut me to the quick. I was devastated. But...he was right. You see, I had always been considered the fun mom, the big ball of sunshine, the one who instigated shenanigans at the most unexpected time, 'the shenanigator', if you will. Now, my kids and my family didn't even want to be around me. I spent so much time in a work environment that changed the very fabric of who I was. It was definitely an eye opener for me. People didn't really count, and because of that I let it affect and change the very person I was. Down to my core. Now, I'm out of that environment and I own my own business. My passion is helping other businesses, no matter how big or how small, take actions that will show their team members how much they truly do matter. They do count!

Notes

1. "How to Get Better at Things You Care About." Performance by Eduardo Briceño, TED, 1 Feb. 2017, https://www.ted.com/talks/eduardo_briceno_how_to_get_better_at_the_things_you_care_about?language=en. Accessed 6 Jan. 2023.

Bonita Palmer

Bonita is a proven leader, speaker, business growth coach, and connector with over twenty-five years in corporate operations management and business ownership. Her focus is delivering exceptional leadership, empowerment, and management practices in customer experience-driven business environments.

Seeing the impact of the 2020 pandemic on so many businesses, Bonita felt compelled to bring that same level of operational expertise to the regional business community. She started BGP Group ActionCOACH, where she is instrumental in making business owners' dreams come true by tackling the challenges they face every day: maximizing profitability, improving cash flow, creating better systems, and finding and retaining rockstar team members.

Working with business owners and their teams, Bonita helps successful businesses create and achieve high-level performance, productivity, and profits. When a business is scalable and sellable, the owner can exit how and when they want. They have the opportunity to enjoy the life they dreamed of when they first opened their doors.

Bonita holds Business and Executive Coach credentials with the Global ActionCOACH Firm. She also has certifications in Business Training, the Harvard School of Business Foundations of Management, and is trained at the Lean Six Sigma Greenbelt level. Bonita has shared her knowledge and insights with hundreds of team members, business owners, and community leaders throughout the region as a keynote speaker and seminar presenter. Her many topics include "Six Steps to Growing a Profitable Business," "How to Hire," "Train and Retain 5-Star Team'" "Five Ways to Massive Growth," "What's Your Exit Strategy?," "Fearless Leadership," and "Power of One."

Connect with Bonita Palmer:

https://www.linkedin.com/in/bonitapalmer/

13.

Unconventional Leadership

Start With A People Strategy

Mike Sipple Jr. | Co-Founder and CEO of Talent Magnet Institute®, CEO for Centennial Talent Strategy & Executive Search

> *The key to successful leadership today is influence, not authority.* – Ken Blanchard

The story of intentional and unconventional leadership is mission-critical right now. As a leader, your actions are not only a **_reflection_** of the entire company but also the **_foundation_** of the company's culture. Yet, far too many leaders are more concerned with how they and the company look on the outside rather than how the culture functions and feels on the inside. The growth and financial gains of the organization too often trump the impact leaders have on their people, and this must change. If you aren't paying attention to organizational health, you can't sustain financial health – the two go hand in hand. So, how do you ensure that you have a healthy team culture? You start implementing a "people" strategy. A "people" strategy is a roadmap to help your business grow. It is designed to encourage widespread, company-wide alignment. Focusing on your people strategy will, in turn, improve employee performance, engagement, and satisfaction, which will give the company better results overall. According to the latest Gallup report, 51% of employees are disengaged in the workplace, while 13% are actively disengaged.[1] Whose job is it to promote employee engagement within an organization? Is it the employees themselves? No. It has to start at the top! Leaders must understand their role in shaping their organization's culture – making intentional efforts to help develop their people. A leader's influence over others can be either positive or negative based on their personal leadership style and execution of strategy. This is why it's important to lead with intention. Your "people" strategy can only go as far as a leader is willing to model.

Every leader impacts...but few impact for the better.

Building a Community of Trust

Let me tell you about a friend of mine who has made intentional, unconventional leadership his natural way of operating and whom I continue to learn from to this day.

Mehmet Yuksek was the President and CEO of Perfetti van Melle North America for over six years. Mehmet had been leading brands, teams, and organizations for Perfetti all throughout Europe. Mehmet was leading a country for the organization in Istanbul, Turkey, when he was tapped to move to Erlanger, Kentucky. He was tasked to begin the next chapter of growth for North America.

Perfetti is the world's largest family-owned confections company, and I've been on the side of helping Mehmet place amazing talent within this organization through my talent and executive search company, Centennial. I have been actively involved in the journey of adding key leaders, executives, and talent organizations to the company. The best part is that once the new talent landed at Perfetti, their career success was just in the beginning phase too. Transformational work didn't just happen for the company, it happened with and through the people. No great business strategy can be executed without humans who are aligned and energized to accomplish that strategy.

Talent is mission-critical for the success of an organization, and it's number one on Mehmet's agenda to create a culture that attracts the best talent. He takes a lot of time to get the right people in the right seats because their success is the collective's success.

Mehmet was tasked with setting the vision, building the team, and creating an organization to accomplish the purpose and vision. We became a key partner in his success. He chose our firm because of our focus on the 4C Recruiting

Process® and our intentional focus on building a team based on Character, Culture, Chemistry, and Competence. Our relationship established a connection and trust that helped us understand his vision and how it could translate into a people strategy.

Seven years ago, I was at a conference for Perfetti, and I was talking to someone new to the team. I was curious about how the "people" strategy was impacting the company as a whole. So, I asked him what his experience had been like so far.

He said, *"I've spent thirty years in sales leadership for some of the largest brands in the world, and I've never been in a company where I felt like I could do my best work."*He went on to say, *"Not only am I enjoying it, but it's the safest place I've ever worked because it's the most aligned company I've ever been a part of."*

There was a sense of great pride and satisfaction knowing that my company had such a great relationship with the CEO who created this type of work environment and helped place this person's manager as well as the manager's manager. This felt like such a great example of how building healthy cultures of leaders can cascade down. It was the definition of a 'mission moment' for me at this point in my career. A mission moment is when you hear the impact and implications your life's work has had on the culture and success of a company.

So, what was behind such a raving review of the company? A high-functioning and healthy people culture that starts at the top and walks the walk. It started with Mehmet and his executive team.

This employee confirmed by saying, *"Mehmet's leadership involves his team and partners in key things. His building of relationships transcends the whole organization and enables us to do our best work."*

Mehmet's approach is all about building trust and knowledge. He is a CEO who sets the tone of transparency and trust throughout the organization.

How do you build this kind of trust?

According to Mehmet, You need to be visible, accessible, approachable, and relatable as a leader to build trust-based relationships.

Trusted Leaders are...

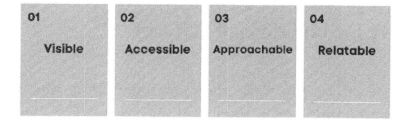

01	02	03	04
Visible	Accessible	Approachable	Relatable

Ask yourself the following three questions to reflect on the levels of trust among your team:

1. What do the people on my team **THINK** when I leave the room?
2. How do the people on my team **FEEL** when I leave the room?
3. How do the people on my team **ACT** when I leave the room?

The answer to those three questions will help inform you of the levels of trust among your team. If your people buy into what you say, they will think fondly of you and your company and, therefore, be on board with your strategy. If they feel empowered and appreciated, they will trust you enough to follow your lead. Conversely, if you aren't present and everyone you are responsible for can keep the needle moving, then the answer is simple.

They trust you enough to show up at their best.

Five Dysfunctions of A Team

If the answers to those three questions above were not answers you'd prefer, then you may be battling a team dysfunction. These are red flags in an organization. In Patrick Lencioni's book, *The Five Dysfunctions of a Team: A Leadership Fable*,[2] he shares the five dysfunctions that ruin team culture.

1. **Absence of Trust**: Teams who lack trust conceal weaknesses and mistakes, hesitate to ask for help, jump to conclusions about the intentions of others, hold grudges, and dread meetings.
2. **Fear of Conflict**: A lack of trust leads to the fear of conflict. In these companies, employees worry more about politics and personal risk management than solving problems.
3. **Lack of Commitment**: When teams become conflict-avoidant, a fear of failure develops. These teams have difficulty making decisions, and they often second-guess themselves.
4. **Avoidance of Accountability**: Second-guessing and a lack of common objectives lead to an inability to develop standards for performance. Team members miss deadlines and deliver mediocre work.
5. **Inattention to results**: When teams lack focus and clear objectives, team members stagnate, become distracted, and end up focusing on themselves rather than the team as a whole.

Reading this list may evoke many different emotions. Perhaps, you read through these dysfunctions and feel really great about where you and your team stand. That's great! This means that you're leading well and have appropriate measures in place to lead a healthy and functional team. Or, maybe you read through this list and feel disheartened. You could be in an organization where one or more of these are eating away at your company from the inside out.

I want you to know that awareness is key and that change is possible once that awareness has been made. Knowing these dysfunctions is important so you can avoid them as a leader. It's also important to remember that you can't just avoid; you must also act. You need to replace this dysfunctional model with one that works!

People Strategy

People strategies boost employee engagement.

Employee engagement is described as "a workplace approach resulting in the right conditions for all members of an organization to give their best each day, committed to their organization's goals and values, motivated to contribute to organizational success, with an enhanced sense of their own well-being."[3]

Do you want your company to have a competitive advantage and be more profitable? Of course! So, you must start with your people strategy to achieve these goals.

The Harvard Business Review Analytic Services surveyed more than 500 business executives, and "71% of the respondents ranked employee engagement as very important to achieving overall business success."[4]

Kevin Kruse, the author of the book, *Great Leaders Have No Rules*,[5] says that employee engagement is not the same as employee happiness. Kruse argues that an employee can be happy and still not be productive. He also says that employee engagement is not the same as employee satisfaction because an employee can be satisfied and still fail to go that extra mile.

So, if an employee is still not engaged, despite the fact that they are happy and satisfied, what does that mean? Engagement means that an employee is committed to the company and its goals.

Let me introduce you to a leadership model that hones in on people strategy developed by my company, Talent Magnet Institute.

Seven Pillars of Talent Strategy

At Talent Magnet, we train around seven pillars of a talent strategy that we call the Leadership Flywheel. These components are what we train leaders with and on to implement within their organization to align their business strategy with their people strategy.

The following are included in the Leadership Flywheel:

1. Attract: we help organizations take steps to attract the right talent to their companies.
2. Recruit: learn to identify and screen employees to hire and create a culture that recruits with ease.
3. Onboard: design a clear and effective process to equip and train an employee to join your company
4. Develop: keep employees engaged and motivated, development is key both personally and professionally.

5. Retain: learn how to keep productive and talented workers and reduce turnover.
6. Ambassadors: create a work environment where everyone thrives and watch your people become your organization's greatest ambassadors.
7. Strategy and Purpose: an understanding of your company's vision and mission are crucial to align your people with your strategy.

When an organization is dialed into these components, your organization is most effective. We envision these components as a flywheel because each is reliant on another. While I could go into each one more in-depth here, you can learn more about this flywheel and becoming a talent magnet at www.talentmagnet.com/fusion.

For the flywheel to generate momentum and magnetism within your organization, it takes everyone's full participation and involvement. That is why a "people" strategy is so important!

Involve Your Team

As the Perfetti manager showed us in my previous example, a team needs to be involved in creating strategy within the company. Everyone wants and needs to feel included and valued – not just for their work contributions but also for their creative contributions.

There are task-focused leaders and people-focused leaders, and to have true organizational health is when the leader is able to combine and utilize the two in tandem.

When the entire team is involved in developing the company's "people" strategy and taking ownership from the ground up, they are far more likely to execute the tasks of the strategy because there is a collective buy-in to the vision.

A good place to start is by encouraging everyone to answer the following core questions...

1. What results do we want to achieve?
2. What is the most important work that needs to be done?
3. Who will complete each part of the work?
4. What is my greatest and best use within the organization?
5. How can I do more of that kind of work?
6. What support do I need to be successful?

These questions need to be revisited and reanswered more than just one time a year at the annual planning meeting. I recommend going through these questions each quarter to be sure you and your team are on track. If they can't answer any of these questions, then have an open and honest dialogue!

Maybe the team knows what results they want to achieve, but they aren't sure what support they need to get there. Or maybe they don't have a clear picture of the direction they are going, and you need to go back to square one to find alignment.

Utilize these questions to lead both yourself and your team well.

It's one thing to have the knowledge of what it looks like to be an unconventional leader, but it's another to put that knowledge into action and implementation and become an unconventional leader. Results matter, but to get the results you desire within your organization, you must prioritize the development and growth of you and your people. Want to get started today? Visit www.talentmagnet.com/fusion for free resources to support you on your unconventional leadership journey.

Notes

1. Amadeo, Kimberly. "How Preventive Care Lowers Health Care Costs." The Balance, Https://Www.thebalancemoney.com/ Preventive-Care-How-It-Lowers-Aca-Costs-3306074#:~:Text=When%20patients%20have%20regul ar%20access,Have%20progressed%20past%20regular%20ma nagement, 28 Oct. 2022, https://www.thebalancemoney.com/preventive-care-how-it-lowers-aca-costs-3306074#:~:text=When%20patients%20have%20regula r%20access,have%20progressed%20past%20regular%20man agement.

2. The Five Dysfunctions of a Team - Executive Agenda. https://www.executiveagenda.com/application/files/3616/ 2085/3781/five-dysfunctions-brochure.pdf.

3. "What Is Employee Engagement." Engage for Success, 6 Mar. 2022, https://engageforsuccess.org/what-is-employee-engagement.

4. Harvard Business Review (2013) the Impact of Employee Engagement on Performance. - References - Scientific Research Publishing, https://www.scirp.org/(S(i43dyn45teexjx455qlt3d2q))/reference/ReferencesPapers.aspx?ReferenceID=1869842.

5. Kruse, Kevin, and Travis Bradberry. Great Leaders Have No Rules: Contrarian Leadership Principles to Transform Your Team and Business. Rodale Books, 2019.

Mike Sipple, Jr.

"Leading with Intention means taking action. I have a gift for you, the people who read this book, because you know that leadership matters." – Mike Sipple, Jr.

"Leading with Intention means taking action. I have a gift for you, the people who read this book, because you know that leadership matters. Visit: https://www.talentmagnet.com/fusion" ~Mike Sipple, Jr.

Mike Sipple, Jr. is the Co-Founder and CEO of the Talent Magnet Institute® and is on a mission to help millions unlock their human potential. Talent Magnet™ is a people-centric leadership and management training organization.

Mike is also the CEO of Centennial Executive Search & Talent Strategy, a half-century of strong firm focused on succession planning and building vibrant leadership teams for companies from over 30 countries.

Mike and his dad co-founded Talent Magnet Institute® after Centennial's clients continued to seek leadership and team development advice from Centennial beyond executive search. Including coaching next-generation leaders, supporting growth in early to mid career professionals, and supporting high-performing teams to lead with intention and create healthy, supportive cultures.

Mike is an Amazon best-selling author of Leadership Fusion, a globally recognized podcast host, and a sought-after guest on leadership, entrepreneurship, and talent development podcasts.

Mike is a sought-after speaker, keynote, and moderator for associations, executive peer groups, conferences, and organizations on the Becoming a Talent Magnet® methodologies and systems, The Great REALIZATION, Leading with Intention, Unconventional Leadership, and holistic approaches to Succession Planning, the secrets to team building, and various other leadership topics.

Mike's insights can be read, viewed or listened to at:

- All About HR Podcast
- Book Smarts Business Podcast
- Hot Mess Hotline Podcast
- Power Up Your Marriage and Business Podcast
- HR Social Hour Half Hour Podcast
- Thrive Global

- Business Courier Leadership Trust
- The Opposite of Small Talk Podcast
- Punk Rock HR Podcast
- Life in the Leadership Lane Podcast
- Impact Makers Podcast
  and countless other publications and podcasts.

CONNECT WITH MIKE SIPPLE JR.:

https://www.linkedin.com/in/mikesipplejr/

https://www.talentmagnet.com/

www.CentennialInc.com

14.

What is in Your Toolkit?

Cultivating Your Personal, Leadership Toolkit

Liz Flynn | Certified Life Coach & Thinking Partner

Congratulations, you are a team leader! You are responsible for your team's production which is measured by the typical metrics; such as quarterly sales goals. For those who choose to do a different flavor of challenging work, you also have the **_opportunity_** to cultivate your team members' potential, – individually and collectively – and develop other future leaders while improving upon your own leadership skills.

You may have come to your leadership role by way of other leadership positions and so you have a frame of reference on how to lead and how to lead **_well_**. Or, this may be your first go-around; you have been elevated to a leadership role by way of success at a prior role. Maybe you were a consistent top sales performer who, because of your high performance, was promoted without necessarily receiving resources for your leadership acumen. Those falling into the latter category may be able to impart sales knowledge or their team may hit their goals independent of leadership.

For example, I once heard an international sales executive say his department was the company's overall top-performing sales team, having seen a tremendous increase in year-over-year sales. Curious, I asked to what this person attributed his team's success. The reply was something along the lines of: **"Me – I single-handedly carry the team and far outperform everyone else."** This prompted me to then ask how he trains and supports new team members. Unsurprisingly, there was no training – new team members are thrown in and sink or swim alone.

Was this team successful? From a bottom line perspective, yes. Was this person a "leader?" It depends on how one views the word and its definition. Neither the fate of any individual team member, nor state of the group dynamic, was a concern to the team leader. However, the top performing team was financially successful for the company and good for the leader's overall career. Thus, we can conclude that leadership and success are not the same animal.

For those leaders solely concerned with hitting metrics with no regard for how your team members develop along the way, this may not be the most valuable content. If you are up to the challenge and self-growth that comes with committing to team-centered leadership and cultivating the best environment for your team members to thrive personally and collectively – let's go!

There are numerous articles, books, and lists of ways to lead a team with no shortage of solid tips, ideas and strategies. Here, you will find complementary content to help you become a discerning leader who delivers your unique business style to your team. By posing many thoughtful questions for you to eventually answer about yourself, the goal will be for you to cultivate a personal Toolkit to ensure your team has their best chance to thrive because you, as their leader, are thriving.

What is a Good Leader Anyway?

If we polled a dozen leaders about what a "good" leader is, no doubt we would get as many different definitions. So, before asking what a good leader is, let's back up and more fundamentally define leader so we can move forward with the same understanding. A basic definition of a leader might be "a person who makes decisions and is in charge of others."

Because we are in search of a **good** leader, the definition we will use is **_a person with responsibility for others, to whom those others respond positively and look for motivation, inspiration, and growth with trust in a predictably safe environment_**.

Taking this further, our "good" leader is: *discerning and self-aware. They know when they fall short and cultivate a toolkit of resources to bridge any gaps in leadership they experience so they continue to grow and lead better.* **A Discerning Leader** thrives in their role because they lead from alignment with who they are in harmony with the team – not separately from the team.

Similarly, before considering what makes a "good," high-functioning, healthy team, let's establish a basic definition of a team as:

> **"*agroup of people who come into contact at work for a particular purpose.*"**

The definition of a good, healthy team we will use is:

> **"*a group of people who communicate well and cooperate to work together towards a common objective.*"**

The **Discerning Leader's** team is further elevated because they are able to operate in a safe and positive environment, able to trust and rely on their leader and each other.

The Road to Yourself

At this point, you may be tempted to ask yourself whether you are a Discerning Leader with a healthy team. Let's back this up as well and identify how to assess the type of leader you are.

In the words of the old Greek maxim: *Know thyself.*

Sounds simple, right?

Some people will have ready answers to the question of who they are, while others will struggle to arrive at a conclusion. If you have answers ready, ask yourself if those answers are honest and true. If you are struggling to answer this fundamental and critical question – or are having trouble answering honestly – the good news is that neither you nor your team is doomed!

To the contrary, your willingness to even ask the questions will benefit you and your team greatly; for it takes courage and shows leadership to be honestly acquainted with yourself. Most people will never summon the courage to even try; instead they will likely spend their time trying to implement a top ten leadership list without understanding whether they are even capable of delivering such tips to their team.

Here are some self-discovery questions on your quest to identify who you are as a leader:

1. What are my dominant characteristics and traits?
2. What are my most predictable behaviors?
3. What are my values?
4. What are my priorities?
5. How would others describe me?

6. The truly brave may consider asking friends, families, and colleagues this question and look for common answers.

Because the **"<u>Who am I?</u>"** question can feel daunting, a different launching point for this self-discovery might be beneficial. Sometimes, it is easier to answer who you are not. Or, at least who you do not want to be. So, if you cannot quite put your finger on yourself, by ruling things out, you will start to see a picture of who you are or want to become.

The good news is, even with input from others, at the end of the day you have to be the one who ultimately answers the question of who you are. And, there is only one incorrect answer. Can you guess what that is? It is an untrue answer. Let's distinguish between inaccurate and intentionally untrue self-assessments.

Can you paint an inaccurate picture of yourself despite your best and most honest efforts? Absolutely. Part of your journey may be the sharpening your self-awareness skills. While it is important to refine your self-awareness, there is a difference between missing the mark with self-assessment because you are not yet able to do so and intentionally painting an untrue picture of yourself because you are unwilling to level with yourself.

Painful as it may be, it is crucial to see yourself honestly – this is a "looking-yourself-in-the-mirror" kind of experience. Once you do, you can begin to work toward becoming the person and leader that you want to be. More good news: the more you do this, the easier it should become!

What if you go through these reflections honestly and come away with a gap between who you want to be and who you are? Perfect. You have done it correctly! Now, you are ready to go on with your march towards **Discerning Leadership** and can start creating a personal toolkit.

Closing the Gap

Let's identify some questions to help close this gap, and then look at a specific example of how to utilize our questions.

1. When am I at my best?
2. When do I thrive?
3. What circumstances (remove comma) or people (remove comma) do I need to have in place around me?
4. What or who do I need to add, edit or remove (replacing delete with remove) from my life to be myself

You may have to think back in your life and remember what was in place and what it felt like to be the person you were when you were at your best.

One person going through this exercise clearly knew he was

humorous, even though he did not feel funny in his present circumstances. He could remember how he felt years ago when he had a more active sense of humor. How did he reclaim this characteristic? He identified past circumstances in which he shined through his sense of humor. For example, he was funniest when he felt confident and intelligent, which he was struggling to feel in his current circumstances.

This led to the question of **_what_** prevented him from feeling confident and intelligent. Both of these characteristics suffered in his work environment. Why? He felt undermined by, you got it, his boss – his "leader." His boss's leadership style was dulling this person's sense of humor. After a detailed reflection of other characteristics this person identified about himself and how he could make those come alive again, he decided he could no longer work for that leader.

Let's pause for a moment and reflect upon an important point. While you may feel out of touch with yourself, you don't need a **_new_** you. You need the **_true_** you. The "**_you_**?" at your best. Which might be obscured by the events, circumstances, and pressures of life. You are still there just as you remember, you just may need to dig a little (or a lot) to polish off your shine.

The questions you asked yourself and answers you identified through this process are discerning questions to help you stay in personal alignment. They are resources to put in your Toolkit to turn to when you feel a little cloudy about yourself. Or to regularly assess what or who you need to add, edit, or delete to be yourself.

Discerning Leadership & Your Business-Style

You may be wondering whether this is too much attention paid to something from which there may not be an obvious straight line to leading your team. If so, ask yourself *"Can I lead others without leading myself? Can I lead myself without honestly knowing who I am?"* Hopefully, you answered both questions in the negative and have bridged this gap in the process for yourself.

In order to articulate or reclaim the true you, you need to identify what questions to ask yourself, how to reflect, and how to bridge gaps; this lays the foundation for additional growth. Only then can you turn to how you lead – your **Business-Style**. Here are some questions you will want to ask yourself as you refine your leadership style.

- What type of leader am I right now?
- What type of environment am I creating for my team?
- What type of leader do I want to be?
- Am I making intentional decisions consistent with the leader I want to be?
- Who or what do I need to help me be that leader?

Similar to being able to identify who you do not want to be as a person, identifying the type of leader you **_do not_** want to be may be the most productive place to begin.

Are you "leading yourself" in your own professional life (with colleagues, peers, and superiors) and personal life in an optimal way? If those leadership relationships are not optimal, then are you able to interact with your team in the best way possible and create a desirable team dynamic?

You may be wondering why the health of your personal or peer relationships is a relevant topic of reflection when considering your team because the dynamics may differ. Consider this: what is a team but a complex, dynamic (as in ever-changing) relationship between people who bring their multifaceted selves to the workplace? The interaction involves personalities, emotions, goals, needs, and desires. These are all influenced by other life factors about which the rest of the team, including you as the leader, may or may not know or fully understand. Does not the health of your team require at least the same attention and intentional work as your other relationships given the complexity?

As you reflect on these questions, let's go deeper and ask, "*Am I leading in a way that is aligned with the true self I worked so hard to identify?*" If not, what do you need to put in place, add, edit or delete in order to bridge any gaps so you are leading from a place of alignment?

A related question that is particularly discerning and crucial to ask, is: "*Am I leading my team the way I want or the way I think I have to lead?*"

This gets to the heart of your company's culture and how it may influence your leadership style and impact your team. I once had a boss that came with some sharp edges and was self-described as mean, but not cold. I spent a fair amount of time deciphering this and decided it meant she had no problem doing what she thought she needed to do, yet did not take pleasure in making hard decisions that negatively impacted others.

At first, this seemed reasonable because of course leaders have to make hard decisions. I let her dictate how I led, knowing she would approve of a "hard" decision as long as I could reasonably back it up because she would make that same decision. Essentially, I mistook aligning myself with her "style" for connection with her and a path to success. In hindsight, I regret some decisions I made that were out of alignment with who I was (and am). I can now see that making a "hard" decision was actually the easy way out as opposed to remaining true to myself and finding another way.

Years later, I was at risk of making a similar. After finally deducing that I was not a cultural fit with the workplace that I was in at the time, I concluded that I needed to alter my approach in order to try and thrive. With the benefit of distance from that environment, I am thankful that I do not have additional regrets that would have come from that personal misalignment as I tried to fit a square peg into a round hole.

Thus, through the hard work of identifying yourself and your preferred Business-Style, you may conclude that you and your leadership style are incompatible with some part of your current work environment. This, then, raises the more complicated question of how one closes the gap between how you are leading and how you think you have to lead in order to fit into the culture of your own boss/leader; or the workplace in general.

Not all decisions are equal and compromises can be made without sacrificing your character, integrity, and preferences. Making a list of non-negotiables would be a solid starting point. You can follow this with a list of decisions or actions that would give you pause. You may not have these at the ready, yet if you start building this exercise into your day either by observation of what is going on around you or decisions you need to make, patterns may emerge.

If you chart out these items and cross-reference who you are, who you want to be, and/or how you lead or want to lead, you can triage the incompatibilities. For example, you may tackle items that negatively impact team members first, as opposed to items that create small inefficiencies or redundancies.

Identifying the Opportunities & Cultivating Your ToolBox

What to do with incompatibilities you identify may be the penultimate question. There is no definitive answer except what you decide for yourself, which may depend on how you see your leadership **_opportunity_**. Even the most challenging situation has an opportunity, although sometimes you have to look closely or from a different perspective to find it.

Here are some general themes of leadership opportunity to consider:

- Seeking additional self-development resources so you can lead the way you want:
  - what do you need to lead in alignment with yourself – a coach, emotional intelligence work, etc.
- Habits to add, edit or delete:
  - what changes can you work on immediately that will benefit your team quickly?
- Interplay between long term goals as a leader versus short term needs:
  - are you sacrificing team members in the short term to achieve longer term success?
- Identifying two sets of deliberate and discerning questions to add to your Toolkit.

The first set are questions to ask routinely:

1. Are my words and actions aligned?
2. What am I modeling for the team?
3. How is the team dynamic and how can I improve it?
4. Do I know each team member and what is important to them in order for them to thrive?
5. Who and what workplace behavior am I promoting and rewarding?
6. What other resources do we need to thrive?

By regularly asking yourself these questions, you will ideally reduce friction-points that arise in high-stakes situations. For example, if team members are not comfortable sharing news with the leader, this increases the chance that things will go off track because honest conversations are not had.

The second set are questions to ask in high-stakes situations:

1. Am I reacting emotionally or responding in a way that enables a constructive plan?
2. How can I support my team through this situation?
3. How can I share in the responsibility for the situation so the team feels we are in this together?
4. How can I improve as a leader from this situation and how can I share that with the team?
5. What is the learning and growth opportunity from this situation for the team so we can prevent it in the future?

To summarize, building a toolkit to support your business-style is most effective as an ongoing exercise. Because whether yours is a team of two, twenty, or 200 you as the leader have a special responsibility to ongoing personal growth and development. This will ensure you can best lead yourself in order to lead your team in a healthy, positive and safe environment so all team members are productive, fulfilled, and – in turn- able to also grow and thrive.

To borrow from Capital One: *What's in Your Toolkit?*

Liz Flynn

Liz has enjoyed a varied background including roles in law, the nonprofit sector, real estate recruiting and, currently, financial services. A common denominator for Liz among these roles has been asking questions to ascertain what is important to other people.

Along the way, Liz adopted a personal practice of posing questions to others partly to avoid sharing personal information about herself. Despite these best efforts, her life journey required personal growth owed to asking and answering hard questions of herself. As a result, Liz now makes more intentional, daily decisions and lives a more discerning life. This has inspired her to obtain her life coach certification.

Liz wants everyone to thrive, especially through the myriad

of life changes we all experience. By being discerning of yourself and identifying the lifestyle you want to live, you can define your opportunity for change and make deliberate decisions aligned with who you really are.

In the workplace, leaders have a unique responsibility to do the challenging work of ongoing personal growth in order to lead their teams in healthy, positive, and safe environments. This will allow all team members the best opportunity to be productive, fulfilled, and – in turn- be able to grow and thrive.

Liz has appeared on the "Building Confidence" podcast hosted by Sue Reid where she discussed confidence and thriving through change. She enjoys spending time with and learning life lessons from her sons, running, riding her bike, living in a walkable community, yoga, native, perennial, pollinator flower gardens, podcasts, lakes, patronizing local businesses, conversation, and coffee.

Connect with Liz Flynn:

https://www.linkedin.com/in/liz-flynn/

Conclusion

Melanie Booher | President, Influence Network Media

Thank you for supporting the authors of *People Fusion*. This book aims to help leaders of small to midsize companies with the tools, tactics, tips, and strategies to build solid teams and retain great people. These fourteen authors have provided their expertise here so that they can influence how we best utilize people and drive business success through people.

Developing and retaining teams can and will look different within every company. By truly understanding your business, your employees, and your business objectives, and goals, leaders can step up to create an environment for success.

There were several themes emerged from the collaboration of authors in People Fusion.

Some critical concepts included:

- **<u>Leading well</u>** – how to become and remain the best leader for your team. Whether you are the CEO,

President, VP, CFO, or manager, it is imperative to lead with intention. The end goal of leading your team to be the best versions of themselves in all aspects of their lives will, in turn, reverberate back into their professional lives. The benefits will be seen and felt by all. When people are happy, they produce great work with a positive mindset.

- **Employee retention** – gathering the right talent to suit your needs as a company leader/manager and to work towards the overall goal(s) of the company.
- **DEI** – there is no question that when companies and businesses are inclusive, by all measures, they thrive. Productivity benefits when many different types of people are included and employed; this inevitably leads to positive outcomes in profitability, notoriety, and overall success.
- **Communication** – communication includes speaking and listening. A strong leader can listen and understand the needs of the people and business and be able to communicate the goals and objectives of the business.
- **Operations & Continuous Improvement** – every leader starts with room for growth. Teams must continue to change, adapt and grow through personal and professional development.
- **Relationships** – connect with your employees and build a professional relationship with them. Getting to know your employees and providing them with the best work environment is a top priority for a strong leader. Professional relationships are key here. Be sure to maintain that there are no favoritism or biases around

your employees.

- **<u>Culture</u>** – recognizing that workplace culture matters to engage your team and keep them happily employed. Are you being intentional with your people by creating a written plan?

As the authors of *People Fusion*, we hope you have found at least a few good takeaways to implement within your business/company.

At the end of each chapter, you can access each author's bio and contact information (website, LinkedIn). If you wish, you may connect with them directly – in fact, we encourage you to do so! The authors are excited to connect and help you achieve your team and retention goals!

As a bonus – it's essential to realize that *People Fusion* is part of a book series. If you'd enjoy learning more from our impressive collection of authors – we urge you to check out our other titles in the "Business Fusion" Series:

- *Talent Fusion*
- *Leadership Fusion*
- *Marketing Fusion*
- *Sales Fusion*

Interested in learning how to get involved with INM or write yourself? Join our free community of leaders at https://authors.influencenetworkmedia.com/ and listen to authors on our podcast: *Book Smarts Business Podcast*.

You can also find us on LinkedIn, YouTube, Facebook, and more!

I'd also like to take a moment to nurture the seed that may be growing within you – to amplify your voice and write a chapter or book of your own! If that's of interest, check out www.inmauthor.com/solo or www.inmaurhor.com/collective to learn more.

If you already have a book – we'd love to support you in taking it t the next level as a speaker, trainer, podcaster, or more! Check out www.inmauthor.com/influencer

Cheers to creating new chapters (in books and life!),

~ Melanie

https://authors.influencenetworkmedia.com

https://linkedin.com/in/melanie-booher

About the Publisher:

We provide publishing & promotional services to business experts who want to become authors.

A media company that provides publishing and promotional coaching and services to authors who write non-fiction books around people in business. Founded by Jodi Brandstetter and Melanie Booher, Influence Network Media is a one-stop-shop to ensure your book is a bestseller and authors are able to use their book as a vessel to their career success.

Our offerings include:

- **Overnight Author** where in two days you are an author of one of our collective book series.
- **Collective Book** Opportunities where you only need one chapter, bio and headshot to become an Amazon Best Selling Author!
- **Solo Bundle** Opportunities for Business Experts who want to write a book that becomes a course and presentation all in one.
- **Micro Book** Opportunity for Business Experts that is less than 100 pages.

To learn more:
https://authors.influencenetworkmedia.com
Publishing@LETSCincy.com

Influence Network Media

Collaborative Book Series

Business Fusion

A Book Series Dedicated to Small to Midsize Businesses and their Success

Launched
August 2021

Launched
January 2022

Launched
May 2022

Launched
October 2022

Launched
January 2023

Book Smarts Business Podcast

Short on time but big on growth? Then the Book Smarts Business Podcast is the podcast for you – the experienced, business professional who loves to listen to podcasts and read business books all in an effort to learn more about his/her profession, become an expert in their field, or maybe even become an entrepreneur down the road!

In 15 minutes, you will learn more about the expert authors, gain amazing insights and knowledge from their unique expertise, as well as the ins & outs about their book, and why they decided to write their book!

For a potential author, Book Smarts Business Podcast provides an avenue for business authors to showcase their expertise and book, and gain more readers for their book!

https://booksmartsbusiness.buzzsprout.com/